The Cat Connection

Front Cover: J.R. in his prime
Back Cover: Digi-Art painting of Columbus by
the Author

ISBN-13: 978-1484076743
ISBN-10: 1484076745

To Karen—
the Cat Lover of,
Poughkeepsie!
may you have lots
more cat enjoyment—

L. D. Matthews
3/13/14

Dedicated to

Smokey, a great communicator whose stainless steel jaw

and permanent Carpe Diem attitude made him a

Champion among cats;

and to Jackie and Kate Gordon,

for their many years of kindness to cats.

Forward

The biggest watershed event in my life was when my wife of 14 years decided that she was tied down and had missed the opportunity to be free. She decided to abandon the marriage and a son, 10, and daughter, 6. She moved a small distance away and in short order married a roving adventurer. The fling only lasted a few months, and in another year I remarried (this time it lasted) but that is another story. In the meantime, my life sunk to a new low. I gave up a couple of houses, most of my furniture and collections, but still had my children, my 1826 farmhouse and my soulmate cat, Columbus, or Cols for short. My dreams of a permanent family, however, were in ruin.

When the children went to visit with their mother and her new live-in, I remember sitting on the front step of this enormous house in the country and feeling that everything I held dear had gone up in smoke. I hardly knew which way to turn. But when Cols sat on my chest that night in bed, I began to understand that I needed some perspective. I began to see current events from his viewpoint. And I began to comprehend that the understanding of life could actually be simple. Little did I know that before this journey was done, for me at least, the veil would be lifted on some of the greatest mysteries.

It was with Columbus that I first made a connection that literally changed my view of life. Not all at once, like some magic wand, but very gradually over a period of years. In fact, when I look back on it, it is very difficult to pinpoint the exact start. It was not something that I consciously controlled or sought; it just happened. Cols liked to climb on my chest when I was lying on my back, a habit he continued to the end of his days. So doing, he would gaze into my eyes, gently claw my chest with rhythmic contractions, and purr softly. I would scratch his ears or his chin, or rapidly drum on his flank (a personal communication we developed to emphasize our connection). After a few minutes I became aware of his feelings and his reactions to my thoughts. This seemed entirely natural to me, and only now, as I try to write down the experience or to explain our regular communication, does it seem to me difficult to put into words so that you would really understand it.

There came a time when I became aware that I could understand his thoughts, and he mine, that we truly could communicate without a spoken language. Today I realize that this happens far more than most of us recognize, between people and other creatures. Most of the time it goes relatively unnoticed, or is unconscious, or both. But it is there, and if you look for it, you can find it. And even improve it.

Of course I am now compressing these experiences in order to write about them. For a long while I just assumed that the whole process was taking place in my head, and that to call it communication was simply to admit that the mind is a very inventive thing, maybe with the aid of a few non-verbal signals. But in time Columbus taught me to understand it differently.

I write about our communication using language, but the process itself is non-verbal. We put language on top of such experiences as a construct, after the fact. For example, assume that you are driving and stop at a red light. If you write a letter about it, you might say "I stopped at the red light." But if you think about the experience, it didn't occur to you using language; you didn't say to yourself, "there is a light and it is red and I must stop." The actual experience happened without language – you saw a light in the distance, perceived that it was red, looked and saw an intersection, then looked for a line marking a place to stop (either real or imagined), looked for other traffic and pedestrians, slowed and stopped the car. There was no need for language until you decided to write a letter. This is a good thing, because language is cumbersome. If you had to translate every experience into language before you could act, it would not be very efficient.

Babies communicate pretty well with their parents and caregivers before they learn language, and a surprising number of ideas and thoughts are put across with relative ease, but since language is well adapted to communicating the basics (food, shelter, hot, cold, etc.) we soon forget how well we could do without it. It is possible to communicate sophisticated concepts without language, and between species. In describing it, however, I am forced to use the written word, so I must ask for your understanding that the words are a forced construct that is one whole order removed from the actual event, and depends on my meager ability to construct the scene.

Anyway, on that dreadful day when my family was in ruins, I went to bed early, emotionally drained. Feeling very much alone in this big house, I went to bed and Cols climbed on my chest. I spoke to him, and as he gazed into my eyes, his answers were clear.

Well, Cols, it's just you and me.
– It's always you and me. There's not as much change as you think.
You are my loyal beast.
– You and I are always one; nothing can change that.
I am glad to have you. I could not ever give you up.
– Try not to be sad; things will work out.
Things will never be the same.
– You are entrapped by thoughts of the past and forecasts of the future. Neither exists. The past is gone, the future does not exist. Learn to deal with the now.

First Cats

When I was young, we had a dog, but it was really my older brother's dog, Spot. There are pictures of me playing with Spot outside a snow igloo we built. And when I was seven or eight we got a cat, Gabriel, who became a legend in our family, and thus has his own chapter.

Gabriel would not have gotten along with the next creature involved in our household. I had been given a camera and was very interested in various kinds of photography, especially closeups and animal studies. We had squirrels on the front lawn, so I got some peanuts in the shell and attempted to lure one up on the front porch, close enough for a picture. I eventually succeeded and the squirrel got tame enough to be named, Loochi Hao.

When Loochi was not fed his daily peanut (suitable for either eating or burying), he discovered a way to get our attention. Our front door had a mail slot with a brass cover. Loochi found that he could lift this cover and let it go with a satisfying clang. We could then leave a peanut in the slot and he would retrieve it. Soon there was a daily "Clang! Clang! Clang!" at the front door. My friends – and probably my parents friends – did not believe the story, but it is true. Loochi rang for his peanuts through several seasons.

I've been an avid reader all my life, so I guess it's not surprising that our next cat's name was also inspired by a book about a creature who loved flowers – Ferdinand the Bull. Ferdinand the cat was so named because of his propensity for getting close to all the flowers and plants in the house and garden. He would sniff, rub against, and even devour anything that bloomed. Truly nuts about flowers. When this happened indoors, as it did on a daily basis, my mother was not always amused. Does anyone doubt that each of these furry creatures has his or her own personality? Live with a few of them and you will see.

We had some other cat and dog guests as I finished my schooling and went off to college. While I was still in college, I remember a cat I had named X23 (I don't remember why the name except that I was preoccupied with science). My mother passed away during my first year of college, so my father and I were "batching it" in a new house in the suburbs, complete with X23 and his companion, a black Lab named Lancelot. X23 was proud to assist in the proper training of the dog, that is, trained to accept the cat as undisputed lord of the household. X23 is memorable because he helped me with my experiments in closeup photography. I wanted to make prints of his face that would be sharp enough to see every hair. I still have a 16x20 print I made myself that does just that.

Gabriel Churchcat

The first cat to make a profound impression on me came to the door when I was seven. At the time I was reading a children's book about a mouse called Gabriel Churchmouse, so it was with the inspiration of a seven-year-old that I thought Gabriel Churchcat would be a very clever name. Regardless of namesake, Gabriel did turn out to be a very clever cat.

Gabe was white with grey and black and came to us full grown, from parts unknown. He wandered in unannounced and decided to stay. (If you have not owned many cats, you might not realize that it is the cats who make these decisions, not the humans.) Gabriel became pretty well known in our family for his remarkable intelligence. He also talked, and made his opinions known without question.

He was uncommonly smart, and like many cats who consider themselves human (or superior to human, I'm not sure which), he could and did open doors and cabinets, and knock on things to be let in or out, talk when he needed something from us. Most important from my point of view, he was a perfect playmate, always ready to play a game. He learned to sit up on command, and always enjoyed demonstrating this for visitors.

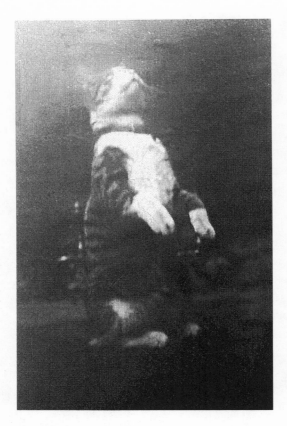

Gabriel, c. 1943

Gabriel taught me the joys of predator play, like
"catch the lump under the blanket". Gabe and I
would play for hours in my bed, cat and mouse or
cat and arm/hand. I learned to endure light bites
and scratches with laughter as I was repeatedly
pounced upon. More than once at night my mother
would say through the door, "Stop playing with that
cat and go to sleep!'. Eventually we would stop
and Gabe would curl at my feet on the bed. We
became inseparable when in the house.

We lived in a big rambling three-story house in Merion, PA, complete with servants' stairway and servants' rooms, which we sublet to a traveling salesman. We were renting, because World War II was underway and it was impossible to buy residential real estate (we had already spent six months living in a suite of rooms on the tenth floor of the Hotel Pennsylvania in Philadephia). Anyway, it was full of rooms – kitchen, pantry, formal dining room, living room, study, on and on – and Gabe and I had a ball. Most of the household had no idea "where that cat has gone to", but I always knew.

I was an aviation buff from an early age, had taken a promotional ride in a corrugated tri-motor with Clarence Chamberlain and watched from my backyard as yellow Stearman biplanes and Pitcairn autogyros cavorted overhead. In the basement, with Gabe "helping", I built models of China Clippers and P-51s and B-29s.

One day Gabriel, no doubt seeking the source of the noise of fluttering feathers, got stuck in the chimney. We couldn't find him and I wandered the house calling his name. Finally I heard him at the fireplace. He had climbed in and gotten above the damper. And did **not** want to come out that way. "Leave him alone", was my father's advice, "he'll come out eventually." Dad was right. I put out some treats. But it was a working fireplace with a filthy flue, and when he got hungry enough, out came a very smudgy cat.

The war ended when I was ten. I remember clearly reading the front page of the newspaper as it announced the atomic bomb, very exciting stuff for a 10-year-old who thought the war was pure excitement, adventure, and heroics. And who had a brother in the Navy driving one of those landing craft into places with exotic names like Iwo Jima.

On a day not long after the end of the war, Gabriel went out for his usual daily walk and did not return. (We never heard of litter boxes in those days. The cats learned to go out, and to ask when they needed to go in or out. Kittens would be started out on newspapers like puppies, then introduced to the garden.). It was not unusual for Gabe to be gone for some hours if he found something interesting. But when he did not return at all that day, I got worried. Next day I scoured the neighborhood and pestered my parents with questions as to what could have happened. "Could he have been run over?". "It's possible, " Dad said, "but we probably would have heard about it." My Mother gently told me that he might have simply picked up with another family, reminding me that, after all, he came to us just that way. But I knew better, Gabe would never voluntarily leave my side.

I was too young to have learned that many pets leave our lives just this way, without explanation, without our ever learning their fate. Gabe remains faithful still in my mind's eye, his memory never dull. He is still a constant companion. We had many other cats and dogs and creatures in our

12

family, but the memory of Gabriel endured, even with my parents. Without doubt, he had become a full member of our family. And he was unquestionably one of my best friends, more than that, the kind of childhood friend one never forgets.

My father was not a cat lover, but he made an exception in Gabe's case. Every other cat I ever had he would refer to as "that damn cat". When he would claim to not like cats, I would remind him of Gabriel, and he would say, "Gabriel was an exception." Consciously or unconsciously, I would compare all future cats to this gold standard in my mind. There really is such a thing as a strong human/cat bond which sometimes develops on a level of unspoken communication and love. It would be many, many years before I had another cat like this.

WWII

I was only seven years old at the end of 1941, but I clearly remember the radio announcement of Pearl Harbor and the start of World War II. My brother was nine years older and could hardly wait to join the Navy after his high school graduation. His room was next to mine and I could clearly hear his morning radio program, "The Dawn Patrol", which featured music by Glen Miller, Harry James, Benny Goodman, and the like.

I lived only a short block's walk from my elementary school in Merchantville, New Jersey at the outbreak of World War II. My brother and I that winter finished a real igloo in the backyard, just big enough for the two of us and our dog (aptly but un-originally named Spot).

My brother was sent to the Pacific as a landing craft driver, participating in many island invasions before returning unharmed and with fascinating souvenirs including a Japanese rifle, bayonet, and hand grenade (empty). But during the war years we had many letters from him, often cut to pieces by the censor. I could be found at the top of my swing set, gazing down the long top piece of the set, which had become the long nose of my personal P-40. I was shocked and not sure of belief when a schoolmate corrected me that the top fighter was now a P-51.

Bobby, my best friend all during grade school years, originally lived next door, had moved to a new house a few blocks away – still biking distance – and was living alone with his mother, which gave us an entire half-finished basement to play in. That is, when we weren't biking all over town with playing cards attached by clothespin so that they hit the spokes of the bike's rear wheel and created a motorcycle sound. Bobby and Mom lived alone because his father was a Commander in the Navy, engaged somewhere in that Great War.

My own father had fought in WWI and had his own souvenirs. Now he was an executive in a chain of grocery stores, which was fortunate for us. Not that we got more points (like red cardboard pennies, needed for rationed food like meat, butter and sugar) or stamps (needed for gasoline) than anyone else, just that the grocers and butchers in the stores would save some of the scarce items for when we came in. I did my part by wheeling my wagon around town collecting newspapers, old aluminum pots, and cans of bacon drippings. These items were turned in, theoretically to make more ammunition. It was also my job to drive a tricycle festooned with red, white and blue crepe paper in the many patriotic Merchantville, NJ parades.

Young people today have a different concept of American wars. They are distant, if violent, conflicts keeping the military and defense industry busy. But aside from casualties, they have little effect on our daily lives. This was very different in WWII when just about every aspect of life at home was affected, including the shortages of staple foods and gasoline.

I had the misfortune to live among a bunch of kids that were four and five years older than I was, and as a result they were always parading their superiority. They tried to tell me that the Easter Bunny was not real, that my parents were really Santa Claus, and that the black stuff sealing the cracks in the cement street was actually licorice. I gave a fair amount of thought to this last one, but decided not to believe anything they were pushing.

We moved five times during the war, first to Bryn Mawr (a wonderful stone house with woods and trails behind), then to various Main Line locations and one six-month stint in the Hotel Pennsylvania, where I was best friends with the lovely brunette elevator operator – and devastated when she got fired.

Of course I played a lot in those Bryn Mawr woods, with and without my good friend Craig from next door, mostly war games. When not in the woods or out sledding the steep drives of a private estate nearby, we could be found lying on the floor of one living room or the other listening to programs like "The Inner Sanctum", with its squeaky door.

My family also took walks on those woods trails, and our cat at the time was unusual in that she would traipse right along with the family, right on our heels. I remember that by the end of the walks she would be panting, and I would carry her the last few yards. I walked a few miles to the train station each day and commuted to school (the Episcopal Academy) by train. One afternoon as I came home from the station, news of President Franklin Delano Roosevelt's death came over the radio. No one had ever heard of his replacement, Harry Truman.

When we were temporarily ensconced in the Hotel Pennsylvania, in a suite with a small kitchen, I was able to get baby-sitting jobs. Also, a neighbor introduced me to chunks of chocolate mixed with corn flakes cereal, formulated to stay together and resist melting, for the armed forces in the hot Pacific territories (these were the forerunner of Nestle's Crunch and Hershey's Krackel). But to me, the great feature of that place was that we were on the tenth floor. Can you imagine how far a balsa glider will go from the tenth floor of an outside fire escape? Marvelous!

Years later, I mused with Columbus that I never had found much insight about wars.

Do you have any insights?
– What you call insight is just a broader understanding
How do I get that?
– Strive to grow your understanding
Do you understand the human concept of war?
– I understand fighting when necessary; it is part of the condition of life, but should not be glorified
Do you anticipate actions that may be needed in fighting?

– Yes. To win, one must think ahead
Do you think it wishful thinking to want to
abolish war?
– We can't change the biological animal, but
perhaps we can avoid destruction

I've been asked if I really believe in these mental connections, if there is a method, and if it works with other cats. The answers are, yes, I came to believe that the connection goes beyond my own imagination, yes I believe the method can be learned by others, and yes, it works with other cats (so far, with about 70% of cats to some degree provided they are not too young or too old). My doubts were resolved after making contact with many new friends in the cat world (and not all owned by me). But I can't predict which cats will have meaningful communications, even among my own.

I have thought about trying to teach or codify a connection method but ultimately decided that it was not appropriate for this book. Perhaps, depending upon the acceptance of this book, a later project.

My Heroes

In high school, I read every book I could find about flying, and carefully studied each issue of Flying magazine, including the ads for the Cessna 140, 170, and 190 (one of which would be my first airplane in a few years). But my favorite book of the time introduced me to my hero for what I wanted to do. "Weekend Pilot" by Frank K. Smith told the true story of himself as a new lawyer who learned to fly, got himself a two-place Cessna 140, and began flying to the seashore from the Philadelphia suburbs. What a wonderful story!

A little more than a decade later, I met Frank Smith at the little field in State College, PA. I had flown my 4-place all metal Cessna 170 into my alma mater to visit friends, and he had come up from Washington in a twin engine plane he called "my half-Aztec" (it was a Piper Apache that had been upgraded to the more powerful Piper Aztec engines). I told him his book had influenced me (and thousands of others) and he admired my craft. We swapped tales, we both occasionally flew in to the seashore at Ocean City, NJ (he was to become very influential at that airport). He had become an aviation lobbyist in Washington, DC and told tales about Congressmen who refused to fly when offered a ride. I can still hear him tell the story, "but I got two fans, I said…".

I discovered a larger-than-life hero on the publication of "Fate is the Hunter" by Ernest K. Gann. This book is an autobiographical tale of the author's training to become an airline pilot, his early experiences on the line – in the days of flying in really messy weather – and then his entry into World War II and flying experiences all over the world. Written in a seat-of-the-pants style with verve and lots of drama and a beautiful command of language, it is still a wonderfully entertaining book to read, and I always recommend it to pilots or budding pilots. I have read and re-read it dozens of times, and have nearly memorized parts of it ("Franko! Full flaps!" is a line that comes to me, about an overloaded takeoff about to crash into the Taj Mahal). "Fate is the Hunter" has remained my favorite book of all time. [1]

I have retained interest in the WWII conflict and learned a great deal more about it in the intervening years. And decided somewhere along the way that my most important hero was perhaps the greatest man of the twentieth century, Winston Churchill. Of course he had faults and made many errors, a few of them extravagant; nevertheless he rallied his country when it was exactly what was needed. He helped bring America into the war, thus saving his own country from nearly certain defeat. And he did all this with one primary weapon – fantastic command of the English language. And the ability to speak it forcefully as well as write beautifully (or more often, dictate, then edit).

He was also a pilot (enjoyed taking the controls of the giant flying boat taking him back across the Atlantic after meeting with Franklin D. Roosevelt) – and member of Parliament – and a bricklayer –

and a soldier – and the top admiral – and anything else he set his mind to.

I love Winston's remark when he was asked if he was not afraid of being severely criticized about the conduct of the war when the history of the conflict was written. "No," he said, "because I shall write it myself". And he did just that. His six volume history of World War II, when published, instantly became the standard classic history of that conflict, and endured in that role. The set is a magnificent effort worthy of the man. Subsequent historians have shown that Winston was wrong here or there, making him human I suppose, but oh my, what a glorious career.

Kooken

I started cave exploring when I was in college. Fortunately at Penn State's main campus in State College there was an official chapter of the National Speleological Society (NSS, an affiliate of the American Academy for the Advancement of Science or AAAS), and after one abortive trip with my roommate (stupidly following the tracks of a mountain lion into a single-passage cave – fortunately the lion wasn't home at the time) we were featured in the town newspaper and the chapter made contact with us. NSS members, by the way, were among the early conservationists, with the motto, "Take nothing but pictures; leave nothing but footprints".

I got hooked on exploring the many caves of the local porous limestone as well as trips to Virginia, West Virginia, Kentucky and Tennessee caves (which tend to be much larger; some require real, even professional, exploration effort). I started the local caving newsletter and continued editing it until I graduated four years later (I spent 5 years there because my newfound cave interest led me to expand my Journalism major to include a Geology minor – most of the cavers in the local chapter were Geologists or Hydrologists or Mineralogists with a sprinkling of Biologists studying strange cave life, adapted to total darkness).

While I was in college, I also developed a strong interest in photography, and combined this into work in the unusual sub category of cave photography, which has its own special challenges and rewards. For example, I found it was still possible to order flash powder such as used early in the century. It was good for huge subjects like Grand Central Station – which really could not be lit any other way at the time – and equally good for huge cave rooms (except in caves you only got ONE shot with flash powder, then plenty of smoke afterwards). I burned one poor fellow's eyelashes off while on a National Park Service Expedition in Wind Cave, South Dakota.

I made one minor discovery while caving in college, in Aiken cave. I don't remember exactly why, but I had my light out and was taking photographs in a small room full of little calcite formations, a room about the size of a bathroom or a train compartment. For some reason, I shut my eyes at one point just before the flash went off (in those days, I was using flashbulbs). When I opened my eyes after the total darkness of the cave, I was astounded to see that all the calcite formations were glowing with a strong green light!

I knew that calcite glowed under fluorescent light, but I had never heard of this phenomenon. I repeated the experiment and got the same result every time. I showed this to my friend Herb Duey, a mineralogist who was working in a different room in the cave. That led us to a long series of experiments, because indeed the phenomenon was unknown. It turned out that cave calcite was sensitive to not only exciting by light (photoluminescence) but also could be excited to glow by other forms of energy, like heat, or even by striking it (thryboluminescence, if I remember correctly). Other forms of calcite don't do this. Herb wrote up the scientific paper that broadcast our findings.

Luminescent section in Aiken Cave, c. 1955

My interest in this peculiar caving hobby eventually led me to become Editor of the national magazine and then a position on the NSS Board of Directors and eventually a Fellow of the Society. But the cave tale I want to tell is my most memorable brush with complete disaster. I was still in college, young, thought I knew nearly everything worth knowing, and confident of my caving and rock climbing skills. To say nothing of expertise in explosives.

In those days it was possible to buy as much dynamite as you wanted, and it was cheap. Farmers used it to blow up stumps and boulders that were in the way. We mostly used it to smooth out trails in caves (in big caves where the passages run for miles, caving parties can push on for 24 hours or more and can become exhausted, so in order to push the frontier of explored passageways, preliminary cave parties would smooth trails and lay in stashes of food and drink for the explorers). We also learned to spend a little extra and get the "headache-free" dynamite, because breathing the smoke from the cheap stuff would give you a pounding headache, and we weren't working in the open air. I did learn enough to keep the detonators stored away from the dynamite. On one trip I was congratulating myself about separating the dynamite as I drove back to my room, only to discover on arrival that I had been **sitting** on the blasting caps.

Kooken, the largest and most demanding cave in Pennsylvania, was located only about an hour west of Penn State, and its location was a guarded secret to protect the unwary (I say "was" because the entrance has been sealed for many years now). Its entrance was in the middle of a farmer's field and began with a dug pit reinforced with railroad ties, then a sturdy locked door. If you had the key (and I did), you could then squeeze down a narrow crack which opened onto the top of a natural pit about 20 feet in diameter. These pits typically had a rounded dome – this one about 20 feet below the surface – and could be 200 feet deep. This one was only about 50 feet deep, ending in a crack that led immediately to a crevice that dropped another good 200 feet. At the top someone had built a heavy wood platform covering the whole pit, except for a square hole at one end, from which dangled a chain ladder down to the floor of the crevice.

We knew that someone had done development in the cave a long time back – I think in the 30's, probably with a view to seeing if it could be a commercial cave (for tourists), or perhaps to see if it could be mined, maybe for magnesium sulfate or guano (high in nitrates used in gunpowder). Whatever the reason, they installed chain ladders, the platform, and numerous crude bridges over the many pits in the cave. There was quite a long string of pits in the last half of the cave (which essentially was one long passage), each pit about 50 feet wide and 30 feet deep, shaped like a funnel and coated with slippery mud, and ending in a pool of very cold water. Most of these had sturdy saplings placed from one side to the other, one for your feet and one higher up to hang onto. Many a caver slipped from these, only to toboggan down the funnel into the water. Not really dangerous, just damned uncomfortable, promising at least a few hours of shivering cold. These stripped poles were still quite serviceable in the mid and late 50's when I was there.

At the very end of the cave passage, about 4 hours steady travel from the entrance, one of our more artistically-inclined cavers had formed a reclining sculpture, in the clay-like mud, of a nude beauty. We named her, but I can't recall what we called her. We had used our carbide lamps to color in the appropriate areas of hair (the acetylene flame, when applied to a surface, would leave a carbon black residue, generally used to leave names and dates in an ecologically friendly manner – cavers were among the earliest conservers of the environment). In the seldom-visited and never-varying environment, she lasted for many years that I was visiting her, without any degradation, and I would bet good money that she is still there and still unsullied. In any case, very few people ever made it to the end of that cave. In addition to being a locked entrance and deliberately little-known, it was a difficult trip and a tough cave even for experienced explorers.

One of the things that separated the casual explorers from the more serious was a sump. After negotiating a 200-foot drop, you came to a huge room (think Grand Central Station again, but cut in half lengthwise). The passage as one entered came into the room near the ceiling, along a steeply slanted side wall. Once you made it to the bottom, you could explore the hard mud floor and a series of mild hills. It was a magnificent chamber. But if you wanted to go farther, you had to dive into the water at one end of the room, swim underneath the rock wall, and know that you could come up into the passage on the other side of the wall. Of course, if knowledge had not been passed to you, you wouldn't know that you could do that at all.

Remember, we used carbide lamps for light. So that meant you had to extinguish your light, wrap your supplies in plastic and go into the water in the pitch dark. After you came up again on the other side and got your breath, you had to slither up the mud bank and get your lamp to work again. All this before you could see the other 90% of the cave (and all the pits), or in fact, before you could see your hand in front of your face! So, as I said, there were not many travelers doing this cave.

Back at the entrance, on the wooden platform, we had become concerned because the dome ceiling above the platform was composed of very friable rock, lots of loose pieces, most small, but some the size of boulders. Some rocks fell on the platform from time to time, and there were always some on the platform every time we visited (usually a few weeks apart). We were concerned because we thought that a large fall of rock could occur at any time, in fact looked imminent, and the platform was old. When the looser rocks finally went and then smashed through the platform, this would strand anyone left in the cave with no way out. So we decided to deliberately blast the loose rock down, then rebuild the platform after it had been destroyed by the rockfall. The main shaft descending into the cave (featuring a 160-foot chain ladder at the beginning of the drop) was offset from the crevice holding the platform, so all the debris would be off to the side and not in the way of the descending shaft. We decided about twelve sticks of dynamite would do the job.

First we thought we'd better block the shaft and protect the long chain ladder by covering this opening with the spare platform planks that were stored to the side in the crevice. These boards were a good three inches thick, a foot wide, and twenty feet long, old enough so the wood was like iron, and were very heavy. It took three of us to manhandle them into position, but when done, the shaft leading to the main room was well covered.

Next we cut the sticks of dynamite into thirds, as we just wanted to drop the rocks that were already loose, not scramble the whole ceiling. We placed the short sticks in strategic locations and wired them up. We used a lot of electric blasting caps and connected some of the short sticks with primer cord (this explodes at the same speed as the dynamite and is used to spread the explosion among multiple sticks). I had learned a fair amount about blasting, including such techniques as placing a mud pack over the stick, for example on top of a boulder. This directs the force of the explosion; otherwise much of the blast force would dissipate in the air. I know it doesn't sound logical that a quarter inch of mud would direct the blast into the rock on the other side, but it works! Finally, we wired the blasting caps together and ran the final wire outside.

Outdoors it was bitterly cold, and it had been pretty cold working on the platform, but hadn't taken us long. I had brought my car to the edge, and it only took a moment to split the lamp cord, trim off the insulation, and touch each piece to the car's 12 volt battery. There was a dull "whump" which I could feel in my feet as well as hear. "Let's wait a few minutes," I said, "I know it's supposed to be headache-less, but I'm not anxious to go into that confined space and breathe all that dynamite smoke." We gave it about ten minutes to clear out and then headed in to see what was left of loose ceiling and platform.

We got a shocking surprise; the loose rock ceiling had firmed up all right and all the loose rock had come down – but **all** of it was now sitting on what we had supposed to be a half-rotten platform! And some of these boulders were the size of end tables, at least five hundred pounds apiece. There had to be 3,000 pounds of rock or more on those old wood planks, and the platform wasn't even bowed.

Now we faced a new problem. Obviously, we could trust the bare platform for a few more years, but all this rock had to be cleared off – and no one trusted going out on it, because, with all this weight, the whole platform might decide to drop at any time. So we had to rig belaying ropes and tie ourselves in, to work. Further, we had to put mudpack blasting charges on top of the larger boulders to break them into small enough pieces to move. We blasted the bigger ones, and still the platform was unfazed. Outside, it got even colder and began to snow, with big flakes.

By the time the smoke cleared, we were really chilled, so we built a small fire at the bottom of the entrance hole, which was open to the sky, hoping that a little of the warmth would make its way down the ten foot crevice leading to the platform. The spare wood from the platform builders was very damp, but we found enough dry kindling outside to get some really hot coals going, then piled the wet wood on top. We began work, and made pretty good progress dumping rock pieces down the platform's square hole. Suddenly, I looked up and could not see my companions on the other side of the platform! In an instant, vision had gone blank.

The cave had decided to inhale, and the fire just outside had gotten very smoky from the wet wood. We began to cough and choke. I immediately went back up the crevice, intending to climb around the fire and up the railroad ties holding the edge of the entrance hole. But the fire was really hot, and there was no way I could get around it. I stumbled back onto the platform. We were all choking and coughing badly. "We have to go down!," I yelled, as I dove through the hole into the crevice below. Of course, the chain ladder was completely blocked by those really heavy timbers. Adrenalin is wonderful…by myself, I grabbed one plank after another and *threw* them off to the side. I plunged down the ladder as the others dropped down behind me.

Previously, for safety's sake, we had always limited the ladder to one person at a time. Not this time – there were four of us on that ladder, with me in the lead. The smoke continued to pour down. I made it to the big room in record time, and was relieved to get out into clear air. From the side, the smoke coming out of the crack at the top of the room looked like a waterfall. But this was a HUGE room, so I was not worried. Surely the fire would burn itself out long before this room would fill with smoke.

The rest of the party clambered down right behind me (a new record: 4 people on the ladder at the same time! – but not the kind of record we wanted to set). We had not dressed for caving and had no equipment with us other than our helmets and two carbide lamps – mine and the fellow who came down as tail-end Charlie so that between us we could light the way for the other two. We perched ourselves on a mud hill a hundred feet from the room entrance and watched the waterfall of smoke pour into the room and pool at the bottom, filling up like a lake.

After a couple of hours, smoke was still pouring into the room and the air was getting nasty. Unbelievable, but we would have to consider going through the sump – not dressed for cave exploring, but clad only in light clothes and with no plastic-wrapped dry clothes, food or supplies – not even an extra charge of carbide for the lamps (carbide lamps run about four hours on one charge of calcium carbide and two fills of water; a notched knob on top controls the rate of water drip, and the water on the calcium carbide stones creates acetylene gas; a spark wheel on the edge of the reflector ignites the gas coming out of the tiny jet hole in the center of the reflector). At least there would be no smoke getting to the other side of the sump, and we knew the cave went on for another mile on the other side, so we would not run out of nice, breathable air. There was, of course, no other way out, so we would have to eventually come **back** through the sump to find out if the smoke had cleared enough to climb back to the surface.

Finally our lungs made the choice for us – we would have to dive into that icy water and proceed in total darkness until we could get a lamp going again on the other side. At least we **knew** we could get through the sump, knew that it only took a minute to get through, and knew that the water level never changed very much. I waded in, swore at the cold, cold water, took a deep breath and plunged under, extinguishing my light. Pitch dark. Swim a few strokes, feel my way upward, stick my head above the surface. Still total darkness, swim what I thought was forward, feel my way onto the slippery mud bank – fortunately not too steep here. Get up on the bank, blow the water out of my lamp nozzle, work the spark wheel until there was a spark, cover the reflector with my hand, wait a few seconds, strike the wheel while withdrawing my hand. Spark, but no light. Try again. On the third try, the hiss of burning gas and **light**!

Those old carbide lamps throw a lot of light, both spot and flood, and your eyes adjust so you can see quite well. It took many, many years for battery-powered electric lights to get good enough, especially in lasting power, to replace the carbide versions for either cavers or miners. And even then, eventually you run out of power. If the cave environment is wet, water can be found, and a pound of carbide will last for days and days.

Now my companions could come through into a lighted room. Eventually we all gathered again on a mud hill and shivered. Still, it was better than being stranded on a mountain somewhere in night and wind and winter. At Pennsylvania's latitude, caves (and ground temperature) stay about 54 degrees Fahrenheit all year long – feel cool in summer, warm in winter (unless you have been submersed in the water). We found it necessary to occasionally exercise to stay warm, since we were all soaked. But there was no wind, and (thank God), no smoke. We elected to put out the lights and conserve our acetylene fuel so we would have light to get out. About once an hour we re-lit a lamp. One guy had a luminescent and waterproof watch (they had radium dials then), so we knew the time.

We talked about everything we could think of to pass the time and take our minds off being cold. We discussed how long it would take for someone to miss us (a distressingly long estimate, since it was known that we planned to work all day, plus it was a Saturday with most of our friends gone on their own trips). We considered how long it might take for the fire to go out and the smoke to dissipate enough so we could make the climb and get out, an estimate we would have to make in the blind unless we wanted to go back through the sump and check the smoke in the big room (no one volunteered).

We finally decided that five more hours of waiting might do the trick, and with luck would get us home by midnight. When the time came, we arranged that

I would go back to the big room, and if I didn't reappear within five minutes, everyone would follow. I dove in and retraced my sump swim, re-lighting on the other side. Much of the smoke was gone, and more importantly, nothing was pouring out of the high crevice that led to the entrance.

We re-grouped and started the climb. It was still smoky, but nothing like before and we made it to the dark, icy winter surface without further incident. It felt really good to get the car heater going and we got back around 1:30 a.m. Of course, that was when – my mind being slightly addled by then – I sat on the plastic bag holding the blasting caps all the way back.

Maple Shade

After college, I moved away from home and lived
in an apartment ("No Pets"). But after a few years,
I bought a house and got married. Then we got two
kittens from the same litter, Nanny and Benny.
Benny was run over at an early age, but Nan not
only survived, she became a long lasting member
of the family. She also became a playmate for our
son. She had her first litter at the foot of our bed – I
woke in the night to a sensation of "wet" at my feet
and a continuously rotating cat down there. She
finally settled and produced 4 healthy kittens,
which we gave away when they got old enough.

*Fremont, our beagle, with the latest batch of
kittens, c. 1965*

At the same time, we had a pet snake, Lucifer.
Lucifer was a boa constrictor and grew to more

than 6 feet before we donated him to a zoo (he eventually lived to be one of the oldest boas in captivity). Neighborhood kids loved to play with him but their parents were aghast. He was, however, completely harmless and let my wife "wear" him around her neck – we used to have great fun going out to stores with him as decoration. For exercise, we sometimes let him have the run of the house. The cats ignored him. When Lucifer got really big we piled him in the airplane and flew him to the Pittsburgh Zoo.

We wanted to live in the country, and found an opportunity to buy a big old brick farmhouse in southwest Ohio between Dayton and Cincinnati. This was situated on 200 acres and featured lots of mature trees, outbuildings, pond, fenced areas, etc. Needless to say, this was animal heaven, not only for cats. We also had dogs, and added chickens, ducks, geese, Black Angus cows, pigs, a pet skunk, ferrets – you name it, all in small quantities.

Benny did not survive long enough to make the move to the farm. But Nanny moved with us, and became just Nan. She had several litters at the farm, which she preferred to raise in the smokehouse (being used not for smoking, just storage). She was a smart cat with a surprising command of English, and loved the outdoor environment that the farm permitted. For pets, this was ideal – they could enjoy the fruits of the outdoors, but if the weather turned really bad, they could go into a barn or come in the big house. Some, of course, were restricted to the barns or a side porch. And some, like chicks and ducks, were raised by us in a room off the kitchen until big enough to go out.

When Nan's last litter was only two weeks old, I came home one day to find her flattened on the road in front of the driveway. She had been hit by one of the fast drivers who used our road as a local shortcut, someone who didn't bother to stop or let anyone know. "Oh, Nan," I said, "I'm sorry, but I'll take care of the kitties." And so we fed the last litter by eyedropper, and all survived. I buried Nan next to the garden, the first of many cat graves on that little farm. It was a sad day for us, as she had been a prominent member of our family for years.

A friend gave us a gorgeous calico, "Callie", who loved to stalk the groundhogs that burrowed around the carriage house – unsuccessfully, of course (but still a great sport). Like many of the farm dwellers, Callie preferred the outdoor world and disdained coming in the house. Even in the dead of winter, there were still plenty of cozy barn spaces. And rodents.

During this time, we also got Avenga, a strange cat, as well as an albino German Shepherd. I was commuting to work 30 miles each way in those days. One fine winter day I came home and heard a strange noise under the hood of my car. I opened the hood, and there on the engine was a rather dirty white cat who had climbed in to get warm. I subsequently learned that Avenga had previously been found several times in people's engine compartments at work. I thought the 30-mile ride on top of the engine must be close to a record, though.

Although a bit greasy, Avenga was unharmed. She continued in the habit, however, and we got used to having to check our engines before departing the driveway. Eventually she successfully bummed another ride and went to live with a neighbor, but I understood she continued her habit. One of the neighbors close to where she went to live was a long distance trucker. One shudders to think where she could have ended up.

We tended to have only one or two indoor cats (really indoor-outdoor, often spending more time outside than in), but in our rural environment we often had as many as a dozen outdoor felines. Typically we would stop collecting at around eight cats. Most of the outdoor cats were quite social and friendly; they just preferred the natural environment. One of these, Murp, was the most outspoken cat I've ever known. No, I take it back, Nefertiti the Bengal was the most outspoken, but hers was in the nature of constant complaint, whereas Murp, a smallish calico, was simply talkative.

Hence the name, as "murp-murp" was her most frequent comment. And she commented on everything – wants, desires, idle thoughts, answering when spoken to, thoughts about other creature's activities. It took me many years to learn to "speak cat", as my wife would say, but these continue to be pretty limited conversations. I can generally interpret what the cat is trying to say, but it usually just involves food or going out or something equally simple. It took Columbus to lift communication to a much higher plane.

Our old farm was a large brick house in two sections with exterior walls three feet thick and many Shaker features like pegs on the walls and two staircases. There were 8 outbuildings including three large barns, a six-stall carriage house, and a cement floored storage building, plus the ruins of a wash house with large fireplace and tall chimney still standing. There was a pond of at least half an acre, with ducks. Although the original 160 acres (one quarter section) was undisturbed, our parcel was carved out of the middle and consisted of 10 acres including the pond and all the buildings. We named it Maple Shade because the house was surrounded by 28 fully mature Maple trees – and yes, we harvested the sap to make syrup. This was a wonderful place to raise children, and animals of all kinds.

The house was originally built for a family with ten children, the youngest of whom had died there of old age not long before we became owners. I found pictures of the house (one with the ten children stair-stepped out front) that dated back to the late 1800s, and others that showed those trees from saplings to fully grown. I had a grand time working with this property, fixing up the house, electrifying the barns, building a dock, etc. I acquired a heavy duty commercial mower and worked at making paths and trails around the pond, out into the fields, and circumnavigating the whole property. These we first used as running paths, then trails for dirt bikes and go carts, then as riding trails for horses.

When my daughter turned 10, I decided this was the perfect time to give her a horse, and found a former state champion Ap-Arab (half Appaloosa, half Arabian) of the same age, a horse that had been pampered by a young girl all her life. When the birthday came, I had the horse hidden in the barn and I made my daughter solve a simple game I had programmed on our home computer. (I was an early user of the home computer because of a wonderful invention called Word Processing wherein one could cut and paste and make all the changes one wanted without having to manually retype the manuscripts!) When she solved the game, the screen told her to "Look in the Barn". Thus was the beginning of a girl-horse friendship of many years, although I also got plenty of cantering fun around the trails. Our barn saw several horses as well as Angus cattle and goats. There was a separate pig pen with a small building and we raised 3 of these, too.

My daughter's horses, Doleigh and ReeseCup, with their winter coats

Our horses always had at least one cat friend. Not so the cattle. The ducks and geese wanted no part of cats, understandably. The goats and pigs were neutral, as were most of the dogs. Occasionally one of the cats would be friends with a dog. At this time we had indoor-outdoor cats as well as some that were strictly outdoor, or barn cats. It was usually one of these that slept with a horse. Somehow barn cats always manage to avoid the hooves of the big creatures.

Our barn cats expanded in number, mostly because people dropped off their unwanted pets (this will be familiar to anyone who has lived in the country). I don't know the exact number, but at its peak I'm sure we had well over a dozen. They kept down the rodent population in those barns and outbuildings. Every day at dinnertime we called them, and they came running for an extra meal. Some were too wild to be touched (although they would happily come when called for food), but most were quite friendly, and some of them followed us around when we did our outside chores; a few of these we named. Sorry, but the names are long gone from my memory.

Calling the barn cats to dinner always gets a response

With long observation, it seemed fairly obvious to me that some form of communication existed between horse-cat friends. Each knew when the other needed help, protection, or just a friendly nose. When one became sick, the other would stand guard and rub against the one needing affection. When one of these cats had kittens in the straw, the horse would permit no interference. I saw this inter-species cooperation over many years with different animals. Both horses and cats can be very social, and sometimes will allow trusted humans to be accepted at the same time, even when there is a crisis. The death of one of these partners would always be devastating to the remaining friend(s), and like us, they would mope around for a long time.

Columbus and I discussed or explored the subject of a possible basis for inter-species communication.

May the force be with you, Cols
– And with you
Is there a life force?
– There is a universality of which we are both a part
How do you find it, or understand it?
– First, become self-aware, then achieve balance with your world
I understand self-awareness; the other might take awhile
– It is not a thing but a constant process, therefore takes your whole life
Sometimes I think you communicate in riddles
– A riddle is what you are calling something of

which you don't have complete understanding
Huh?
– When understanding comes, there is no riddle
Do we understand each other?
– Many times, but not always
Do you communicate like this with others?
– Yes
Who?
– Other cats, sometimes other animals, sometimes another human
Can you give me examples?
–– No. I do not keep track. I am not built that way.
So, your awareness is only of the now, not the past.
–– For me, there is no past in the way you mean, that is, specifics
How do you aggregate your experiences, then?
–– I know them when I meet them

Columbus at the Farmhouse

The Maple Shade parcel was 10 acres carved out
of the middle of a working farm, complete with
barns, carriage house, pond and tracks for riding.
Columbus came to us in 1970 at the age of 8,
brought by two girls of our acquaintance who were
moving into a new apartment which did not accept
pets. A big, heavy grey beast with luminous golden
eyes, he already had his name and unconquerable
attitude. I had no clue that he was to change my life.

We had other creatures – horses, cows, dog, house
cats, barn cats, goat, and geese, plus two small
children. Columbus considered himself in a totally
different category and this was soon proven
accurate. He began pretty much like any cat with
house privileges by taking turns sleeping on each
human's bed. But before much time had passed, he
bonded to me and preferred my chest or leaning on
my feet when in bed.
The master bedroom is on the second floor with
windows on two sides, and the windows on one
side overlook the roof over the side porch. This is
overhung by a big limb of a large tree in the side
yard. I started to call him Cols for short. Cols
quickly discovered that he could climb the tree,
leap onto the porch roof and saunter up to a
bedroom window to ask for entrance by banging on
the glass. Soon his normal entrance and exit were
through a bedroom window. It didn't take him long
to get us trained, and he would conventionally go
out in the evening and want back in at 11 or 12.
When the weather was decent, he spent most days

outside, too – it is a wonderful location for a cat to prowl.

Columbus in his prime

He amused himself by first establishing firm leadership over all the other domestic creatures to be found, and hunting the wilder ones.

In our family, in addition to living for 31 and a half years, Columbus is famous for: tearing off my lip, getting drunk on catnip at each Christmas, treeing a German Shepherd, opening doors and cabinets, and guarding turkeys. Well, I guess those deserve a bit of explanation.

One night while peacefully asleep in my bed, Cols came in and settled on my chest. A few minutes later, I rolled over, and – AAAHHH! GREAT GUMPFH! GET THIF CA OFFA... When Cols found himself being dumped off the edge of the bed, he instinctively reached out a claw and…hooked it through my lower lip. I awoke to a 12 pound cat dangling from my profusely bleeding lip. My slurred roars woke the whole house; my wife thought I was having a heart attack. I gingerly peeled off the offending claw and Columbus looked for someplace more peaceful to spend the night.

At the farm, each Christmas without fail, we would give Cols some catnip spread on a newspaper. Now, almost all the cats we have owned have been uninterested in catnip, aside from a few forays when kittens. But Cols at Christmas, after spending some hours watching the rest of the family enjoy themselves, would roll around in it and get thoroughly inebriated. The farmhouse is large, and if you come in the front door, you can cross the living room in 30 feet, then 15 feet of hall at the bottom of the stairway, 20 feet of dining room, then another 10 feet as the width of the kitchen – quite a long way in a straight line. Cols would start at the living room, dash madly at full speed all the way to the kitchen, put on the brakes and slide across the polished wood floor, bounce off the wooden cabinet with a bang, reverse course and speed all the way to the front door, again sliding the last few feet and hitting this with another bang. He would keep this up while we howled with laughter, finally collapsing into the smallest gift box left on the floor, always something much smaller than could accommodate his massive body. Into this he would curl tightly for a nap. This became a very famous exhibition in our family.

Columbus with Christmas ribbon...

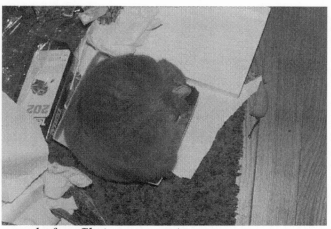

...and after Christmas catnip

Columbus feared no animal, including large dogs. I was afraid that someday he would meet up with a real cat killer, that he would meet an animal more than his match. During his life with us we had many dogs of our own, including Labrador, Dalmation,

German Shepherd, English Bulldog, and several mixed breeds, as well as visitors like the Malemute that came for a week. Cols instructed all of them as to who was boss at the farm (and got surprisingly little argument). It goes without saying that other cats on the scene were even more quickly put in their place, as well as lesser creatures.

One day I looked out the window just in time to see Columbus chase our white German Shepherd right up into a small tree. There was this giant dog incongruously perched in the lower branches. Wish I had a picture. But this hardly even counts, because that particular dog was a wuss who I think had been mistreated as a pup before she came to us. Something much more impressive happened the following year when we had no dog at home.

Our nearest neighbors a half mile down the road had a young German Shepherd who was known as a terror for cats, and we were warned that this dog was a killer. I hoped to avoid any confrontation and could sometimes hear, across the pond to the north, the frenzied barking of this beast as it cornered something. One day this terror got loose and loped up the road to our driveway, which was several hundred feet long with a 90-degree turn in the middle. He bounded in, growling and barking up a storm, and headed for the house. I happened to be on the second floor and peered out the window to see what the commotion was all about. When I saw this big dog, my fears returned, because Columbus was sitting at the very end of the driveway on the walkway to the house. I didn't have time to do a thing, it was all going to be over in a moment. I could just picture this great beast shaking and snapping my cat in two.

Columbus did not move a muscle, just sat there regally as this very large dog bounded up the driveway making a terrific racket, obviously saying, "I'm going to kill me a cat!" The dog reached the cat and put on the brakes, stopping abruptly. I think the dog was a little confused, no doubt never having encountered a cat that did not run or climb the nearest tree. This one never twitched. But as the dog opened its mouth for one last enormous bark of intimidation, right in the cat's face, there was a blur of motion so fast that I could not see it even though I was paying very close attention.

Suddenly the dog did an about-face and ran, the barks having changed to painful yelps. Apparently Columbus had shredded its nose. And as the dog ran at ever greater speed out the driveway to the road, Cols was right behind, taking swipes at the back legs. Cols stopped at the road – I could almost hear him saying, "and don't come back!". I collapsed in relief and laughter. And the dog never did come back.

Columbus and guests

Cols was well known for opening cabinet doors (to check for mice, of course), but also became skilled at opening full-size doors with ordinary round door knobs. He would stretch out full length to reach the knob with both paws, then rotate it until the door opened. He did this not once or twice, but regularly. I've never seen another cat accomplish this – whether because they lack his intelligence or just don't bother to try, I couldn't say.

Columbus was a definite fan of poultry. One evening we had to entertain a business associate that we didn't really like. This gentleman's wife was particularly annoying and had little yapping dogs that were always underfoot when we visited their house, which we did as little as possible.

She also disliked cats. So, for this occasion we built a fire in the dining room fireplace (this is an 1826 brick farmhouse with 7 working fireplaces) and set a formal table complete with a child's raised chair just to the left of my place (and just to the right of our lady guest). We explained that this was Columbus' chair, that he always got a place at the dinner table. The menu was for Rock Cornish Game Hen, which of course got Cols' full attention. He dutifully sat on the chair (even though he never had done so before) and leaned farther and farther toward the main course. Our lady guest was mortified, even though nothing else happened (I gave Cols a reward later).

There was one species of bird that Cols was especially crazy about – turkey, in any form. If we bought a turkey, he would soon figure it out, and if there was a way to get to it, he would be there. We could not leave a table unguarded if any turkey items or scraps were there. We learned that even a frozen turkey was not immune to his sleuthing capabilities. One day we put a frozen turkey in the bathtub, only to return a little later and find him gnawing at it. We learned to put frozen turkeys in the master bedroom bath, close the glass shower doors, then close the bathroom door and block it.

When we cooked a turkey, he would claw our legs and beg and plead and drive us nuts. We probably were at fault for one day asking him if he wanted turkey, but whatever the case, we soon learned that he knew the word. We could not mention it in conversation without having a big reaction from him, even when it was not on the menu. So we started spelling the word, like you would with a toddler. Within a very short time, we discovered that he could spell it, too! We could only get part way: "t-u-r-k..." and Cols would be yowling. This was one smart cat.

My son Kevin had come back to live with me and I remarried, this time permanently. When Kevin went away to school I decided to send an audio message from home in the form of a cassette recording. I began by turning on the recorder and asking Cols if he wanted some "t-u-r" and got some loud responses. Then we cooked a turkey and I gave him a turkey leg. Next I set the recorder on the floor, took hold of one end of the leg bone and said, "MY turkey leg! Give me my turkey leg!" The growls that ensued were truly worthy of a full size lion. And he did NOT let go. He put a paw on the leg between me and his mouth, all the while chewing, "grow-ow-ow-owl." My son used the tape to bolster his tales of Columbus at school.

Solo

By the time we moved to Maple Shade, I was working on my pilot instrument rating. One big advantage of the farm was that it was only a few minutes from the county airport with its 3,000 foot paved runway. I had learned to fly a few years before flying from a little grass field a few miles farther away in the bend of the river, South Dayton airport, and got my license in 1964.

I learned on a little fabric 2-seat Aeronca Champ and it was a wonderful time. Once when my instructor and I were at 3,000 feet above the field getting ready to end the lesson, we could see a big front coming in from the west where it was very dark. So Oscar, my instructor – we called him "Big O" – told me to drop down and land. I cut the power back to idle and setup the normal 70 mph gliding speed. We sat there facing the storm to the west, the engine just ticking over at idle, but there was so much lift in the air, the plane did not lose a foot of altitude. For minutes we sat there, facing into the wind and not moving much in the freshening wind, but the plane simply would not give up any altitude. This is like a sailplane, I thought. It was really strange to sit there without power and have the altimeter stay steady as a rock. Finally Oscar sighed and said, "give it to me." He then stood the airplane on a wing, a full 90 degrees and bent it around so that it fell away and gradually turned all the way around and landed mid-field.

The next day, Big O had me stay low after takeoff,

over the farmland at about 100 feet, and follow the river south to a branching stream, then told me to follow the stream, which was meandering all over the place. So I set a course that averaged the direction of the stream. "What in Hell are you doing?" yelled Big O. "Following the stream," I said. "NO, NO, I want you to STAY OVER THE WATER!" Finally I grasped what he wanted, he was after lots of steep turns without losing any altitude. I didn't have any to lose, I guess that was the point. I wrapped around the curves one hard turn after another, first left, then right, then left again. The entry he put in my logbook for the day reads simply "low work".

Who can ever forget their first solo? After little more than six hours of dual instruction and a decent landing, Big O bailed out of the back seat and told me to make a circuit and then go off on my own for awhile. Without his substantial weight behind me, the Champ virtually leaped off the ground and I made a circuit, my feelings soaring above the airplane, then a smooth landing, touch and go, and out to the practice area to enjoy my newfound freedom. When I returned they cut off my shirt to add to the collection on the bulletin board, emblazoned with my name and the date.

South Dayton airport was a marvelous place and time, a grass haven for the nation's largest collection of Waco UPF-7 biplanes (and an F-5) and some wonderful WWII pilots. I spent some happy years here, learned a lot about airplanes and airplane construction, and airmen. They are all dead now, but their ghosts live on in my memory.

A few years later, I could have used some of that extra lift when I flew my all-metal, 4-place Cessna 170 taildragger[2] out to California to attend a caving convention. I planned a low route through the mountains, going south around Albuquerque. And for the highest pass, we would need to be around 13,000 feet, so we departed at 4 a.m. to get the coolest air. My wife and I picked up another caver in St. Louis, so with lots of caving and camping baggage we were fully loaded. I had the standard metal cruise prop which gave an excellent cruising speed for the trip, but I knew that most people who lived in the west equipped their airplanes with climb props, giving more efficient take-offs from high altitude fields in exchange for maybe 15 mph slower cruise. The best bet is to have a controllable pitch prop, but that meant a much more expensive airplane (I would get to that state eventually, but not for some years).

In winter, frost on the wings will ruin lift, but it is usually fairly easy to get rid of it before takeoff – on cold days it is nearly always there if the airplane is tied outside. I have often had to bring the ship into a warm hangar for half an hour to wipe it off. But in summer, just plain heat robs the air of its lift, and the hotter it gets, the worse the effect. Nothing beats nice cold air for lifting power. There is a double effect, too, because not only does the wing lose lift, the propellor suffers, too – after all, the prop is just a small rotating wing. On top of this, lift diminishes with altitude as the air gets thinner, hence the term that an airplane has a "ceiling". With light planes, once you get above 10,000 feet, there is little lift left, and it takes a long time to claw up to the maximum, maybe 13,000 feet or so (that's as high as I ever got "Alphie").

Of course, the lighter the load, the more the climb performance, so one good way to counter these effects is to lessen the load. But we were close to maximum weight with three people, full fuel, and full baggage. Also, the plane was 16 years old, a 1950 model; while in top condition, it would never be as good as when relatively new.[3] Now we faced a horrendous combination – cruise prop, full weight, high temperatures, and high altitude fields. Leaving early in the morning, we could avoid the worst of the temperatures. But when we stopped to refuel mid-day, the only thing we could do was pick an airport with as long a runway as we could find.

We had to struggle, but we got through the highest mountain pass OK. Now we faced only one more mountain challenge, crossing the Sierras, far ahead of us going into California. So we planned to stop at the airport on the rim of the Grand Canyon, and to take our own little tour out in the canyon itself. The problem was, by the time we refueled, it was noon, the temperature was in the nineties, and the field was above 5,000 feet.

There are charts to compute takeoff distance considering the variables and I checked, allowing some extra distance for the age of the aircraft. It was a pretty long paved runway and the charts said we could go. I picked a marker about two thirds of the way down the runway and promised myself that if we were not airborne by then, I would abort the takeoff. I'd done this once before on a grass strip in the mountains of North Carolina, and actually **did** abort – on the second try, applying full power before even swinging onto the runway, I had finally gotten our fully loaded plane in the air and over the trees with room to spare.

I did one other thing this time – I leaned the engine out for maximum power. At altitude, it is necessary to lean the mixture to get the most out of the engine, and it is common practice once settled for cruise. But you always went to full rich before landing to be sure that the engine would not starve when it was needed, especially after sitting at idle on the approach. You did not normally lean for takeoff because at full rich the engine ran much cooler. But these were special circumstances and I needed as many horsepower as I could get. The method was a little crude by modern standards (where you use an exhaust temperature gauge to precisely find the right point). With the old ships, you did it by ear. The engine rpms would rise slightly at the leanest point before starving began to sound thin, so you listened for the rise, then richened the mixture just slightly from that point.

So I checked for traffic, swung into position at the bitter end of the runway, closed the windows, ran up to maximum power against the brakes, and let go. Alphie (so named for the last letter of its registration) surged normally down the smooth pavement, reached its normal flying speed and stayed there, as expected in the hot, thin air. The tailwheel came off and I held the tail low for maximum climb attitude. No flaps, that would slow us too much. We lifted off just before the marker I had picked for shutdown, so I thought we had it made.

But the airplane refused to climb! We sat there, just above the runway, well below the level of the tall pine trees at the end, and would not climb an inch. What a strange feeling to have the throttle firewalled, the mixture perfect, the controls and speed exactly where they should be, and to think to myself that there was absolutely nothing I could do to improve the situation. Not enough room to land, nothing to do but wait to see what happens. A turn would only lessen the wings' lift. I thought about applying full flaps to try to bounce up – a trick I later used in the mountains of Pennsylvania when going off a short strip with full load – but the flaps on this old craft were the early narrow type and provided little lift, mostly drag.

There is an effect of physics that we were stuck in, called "ground effect". It is simply extra lift between an airplane's wings and the ground, sort of a tunnel effect from the air moving between the two surfaces. It roughly applies the distance of the plane's wingspan from ground up if you imagine the plane turned on its side. It's usually of benefit to pilots because it means you have more lift (and need less speed) when landing. But here, it worked against us, because it lulled us into complacency by allowing us to rise in the air – but only for the height of ground effect.

Just as I was thinking that I should rudder between two trees and was imagining that the landing gear was about to tangle in the upper branches, we sailed just barely clear of the tree tops and started to climb in the cooler air that the trees provided. I aimed for where the ground fell away and muttered my relief.[4]

We followed this up with a fantastic trip over the Grand Canyon at the level of the rim, but miles out to the side where few ever see it. Then we followed the river, past Lake Havasu and the Hoover Dam, landing at Las Vegas. The next morning we again needed to get altitude to cross the mountains, so we cruised back and forth over the cliffs like a sailplane, waiting for rising air. Eventually we got across and into California, and before we returned, we packed up a bunch of stuff and shipped it back so we would have a lighter load.

The dogeared photo of 9288A, or "Alphie" for short, that I carried in my wallet for many years.

Altitude

We had solid clouds all the way over, although no precip and no problems, and plenty of ceiling when it was time to land. Now, on the way back from my Kevin's school in Virginia, things were a little more serious. We had been in the solid grey for quite awhile, and it was a bit bumpy (and I suppose there were some pretty good gusts of wind making those bumps). 93Charlie was providing her normal, solid, secure roar, very stable even in the stormy wind, although some of the stronger gusts were enough to dis-engage the autopilot (really just a wing-leveler rather than a full-fledged autopilot, but still good for resting your hands and arms). She was a leased 182RG (RG for "Retractable Gear"), a solid 200 mph airplane that would carry virtually everything you could get into the cabin and baggage area, unlike many so-called 4-place airplanes of the time, and do so with impeccable manners. But now someone turned on a firehose directed at the windshield right in front of us, full blast, and it roared louder than the engine and went on and on. How can the engine keep running when it inhales all this water? But it never missed a beat.

I kept an eye on the temp gauge up in the right rear corner of the windshield next to the air vent, because icing was very possible, and ice is something a lightplane is not equipped to handle. Small aircraft fly at altitudes where ice is encountered, and a very small coating of ice can completely destroy the lift of the wings or the function of the propellor. Pick up a little ice, and you will go down; the only question is, how far. So when you find icing conditions, best try another altitude – lower if there is warmer air. Higher works, too, because you can get into air that is too cold to form ice – the moisture has already frozen into ice crystals before it encounters your airplane. Of course, if you've already started to get ice, you may not be able to climb higher. And in this case, lower meant running into mountains. So when the gauge showed a rapid drop down into freezing air, I asked for a higher altitude, and got it. Up we went to 10,000 – about as high as I wanted to go without oxygen (above this is not even legal without oxygen).

We had gradually ascended from 6,000 to 8,000 and now began our somewhat more sluggish climb to the new approved level. We did have a small but steady rate of climb, but then we lost all ability to ascend as we were pummeled a second time, this one even louder. Hail! And so much hail that we could not even make ourselves understood by shouting. Hollow aluminum being struck by massive amounts of sizable hail at close to 200 mph makes for one pretty incredible drum! And we were *inside* the drum. We couldn't go down into serious icing conditions, so all we could do was hang on and hope to fly out of it. After a few minutes, we did, and finally were able to resume our climb. At 10,000 we got above the massive cloud deck, although just barely. Up above it was nice and sunny and beautiful. And no ice.

Now we faced the most challenging instrument

approach of my flying career. I was beginning to get to know this particular approach pretty well, but it was never easy. My wife had a consulting job installing a specialized system of computer software on a mini computer for a large mental health center in Gallipolis, Ohio (at the time we lived at the opposite side of the state, in the country between Dayton and Cincinnati). So on the way back west from Virginia, we came to the town shortly after crossing the mountains,

Gallipolis sits on the low flat land next to the Ohio River, and like most big river communities, it is frequently fogged in. The airport at that time was unattended, a single narrow strip, its only facility for an instrument approach a lonely low power non-directional beacon a mile or two away. In the years when I flew, the most challenging of all approaches was the non-directional beacon, or NDB approach. This is because it is not a precision approach and makes no guarantee that you will find the runway at all, unlike approaches that can lead you right to the asphalt. It is essentially static and just sits there and broadcasts a low power beacon in all directions. Still, it is a cheap way to provide for an instrument approach where otherwise there would be nothing, and no way to get in when the weather was even moderately bad. It depended entirely on the careful work of the pilot.

To make such an approach, you first tell the Center what you are doing, navigate into the general area and tune in the beacon. The instrument equipped airplane of the era had an instrument with a compass rose and a pointer that swung all around the face of the dial. When tuned in, the pointer would point towards the beacon. If you turn the airplane so that your compass course matches the pointer, you will be traveling towards the beacon (which could have been *behind* you when you started). You fly until you cross the beacon, which is shown by the pointer abruptly reversing direction; the beacon is now behind you. When you cross it, you start a stopwatch or mark the time on your clock. Everything now depends on your precise navigation in the clouds or in the dark.

You now want to fly away from the beacon on a specific compass heading for a specific time, generally a two-minute leg. You then turn at right angles and fly a second leg for another two minutes. Finally, you turn onto final leg which should point you at the beacon on a course that will also theoretically take you to the airport. You also must manage descending to specific altitudes and reduce speed. This time when you cross the beacon, hopefully on the correct course, you must slow the plane to final approach speed and descend to minimum altitude, and start looking.

Instrument approaches are published as drawings called "plates" which contain all the information you need for the approach, and for what to do if you have a "missed approach"; that is, courses and altitudes away from the airport to set you up for another try if you don't find the runway. In the case of the NDB approach, this means going back to find the beacon again and starting over. The plates always provide minimum altitudes, and non-precision approaches like the NDB have higher minimums, so if the airport is really socked in badly, with the cloud bases maybe 200 feet above the ground, you won't get there, or not legally.

A lot of accidents in instrument weather conditions, maybe the majority, happen during what are called "busting minimums". This happens when the printed approach says the minimum altitude for carrying on is, say, 400 feet, and the pilot reaches 400 feet and still can't see anything. It is very tempting to carry on for what you might tell yourself is "just another second or two" to see if visibility suddenly breaks. Isn't it getting lighter, shredding a little, isn't that the beginning of a glow? After all, no one will know you came a little lower. Meantime, the plane continues to settle lower and lower.

Modern precision approaches (at bigger airports) can literally bring a properly equipped airplane all the way to the ground. A Category III approach can even link to the autopilot and actually *land* the airplane without input from the pilots. But we're a world away from that as I try to find the little Gallipolis strip in this fog of solid grey cloud, working hard to keep my navigation as precise as I can. A few degrees off course (which is *very* easy to do, the Directional Gyro – which precesses and slides off on its own compared to the wildly swinging magnetic compass, and the DG can only be read to about two degrees accuracy; add up all the factors that so easily go off and there could be a sizable error beyond my control), a few seconds off in my timing, or, worse, both of them off on the worst side, and I would be *way* off to the side. The approach I describe assumes still wind; in actuality there is almost always some wind, sometimes winds of various speeds and various headings at different altitudes; these affect the actual course the plane covers over the ground, and thus there is another unknown in the equation. The wind is most critical in the final leg approaching the runway, but generally the instrument indicator will show the pilot that he needs to push a rudder and crab more into the (now apparent) crosswind. Single pilot IFR (Instrument Flight Rules) can be quite difficult at times and sometimes terrifying; long easy periods punctuated by periods of way too many chores compressed in too little time with tasks snowballing beyond your ability to keep up. This kind of approach is not for sissies.

I've crossed the beacon again, changed course and swung right, headed I hope for the runway. Lower flaps ten degrees for more stability, and slowed to 90 mph, wound the trim tab to take the pressure off the wheel. Keep the needle straight, pointing back at the beacon on the reciprocal of the correct course, now it starts swinging a bit, so I add a touch of right rudder to bring it back, apparently there is a bit of wind from the right. Start my final descent, stabilized the rate at 200 feet per minute. Start including the view out the front in my instrument scan – still nothing but whitish grey, flecks of cloud ripping apart and rushing by. Watch the altitude, coming up on minimum, still no ground visible or even a darkening outside that would presage some earth showing up. Reach minimum altitude, stop the descent, get ready to climb out but hold the minimum altitude for another minute. There! Almost directly in front, the runway, but I am already a third of the way along it and way too high to land. I pour on the throttle, retract the flaps, set the angle for normal climb, stabilize the speed to proper climb setting, begin the turn as shown on the approach plate, while pressing the mike button on top of the wheel and announce to Center, "93 Charlie, missed approach". Center approves another try, laconically. I don't think there is much traffic around here today, no one else is mentioned in the area.

IFR rules require us to carry enough fuel to get to our destination plus another 45 minutes' worth to get to an alternate field, and we have to specify an alternate when filing our instrument flight plan. This after checking with the flight weather gurus to pick an alternate that should have decent weather and still be no farther than 45 minutes from the desired destination. This is supposed to keep us safe, but of course things don't always go according to plan, and even the best rules sometimes don't work correctly. To take just one example, the weather gods have been known to slam both your destination and your alternate while you are on the way, and this can become very inconvenient.

But today, my eventual final destination – after

hopefully letting off the wife – is in the clear (Montgomery County, south of Dayton, Ohio), and I have plenty of fuel to get there. I am already past the huge cloud deck that has hung over the Appalachians for days, and only the low-lying river field at Gallipolis has leftover low cloud. So I bend around for another try. I hate making these wearisome NDB approaches! But this time when I cross the beacon the final time I slow up a lot more and use another notch of flaps, and this time I see the runway in time to drop in for a nice landing. I drop off the wife, take off and in another hour the plane is home.

Columbus at the Shore

A friend called and told us about neighbors who had moved but left their young cat behind. The cat was now hiding under the porch at the empty house and would not come out. So we went over and the cat came out immediately. We didn't know his previous name, so he became Nermal. This was one of those cats with a sense of humor (oh yes, it is much more developed in some cats than in others). Nermal delighted in feline versions of practical jokes played on humans as well as other animals. For example, he would hide on a tree branch above the path to the side door, and as you passed, he would leap down on you with all four legs splayed uttering a challenging yowl. When you exclaimed some oath, he would put his ears back and run off, grinning. Life was never dull around Nermal.

Nermal

One day Nermal did not come for dinner, nor the next day. We searched around the farm but could not find him. But a couple of weeks later we found out what happened when we looked into an old abandoned well way at the back of the farm. It had been boarded over, but one of the boards had rotted, and sadly, Nermal had fallen in and was unable to get out.

After more than twenty glorious years on our old farm property and with our children pretty well grown, it was time to move to less demanding real estate. In 1985 we decided to move ourselves, cats and dogs to the Eastern Shore of Maryland, where my father was born and where we still had some distant family. This was a laid back area that still felt like living in the 50's, and we found a nice spot out in the country along a deep river emptying into the Chesapeake, partly chosen to accommodate our small sedan flybridge boat, previously docked in Lake Erie.

We moved in the heat of August using a large U-Haul truck towing the boat and followed by one of our cars. Columbus, already 22 years old, rode with me in the front seat of the truck but at a stop mid-way when we put him on the grass he had the dry heaves, obviously heat stroke – so we moved him to the air conditioned car, after which he was fine. Our daughter Jenny was ready to start high school in a new environment.

The cats Jenny and her friend got from the dump lived with us as outside cats. We fed them and arranged places for them to seek shelter in bad weather, but they were essentially wild. One had a litter and we started to call her Mama Cat. After the second litter we decided to have her spayed, and we kept one of her kittens from this last litter – named Pocohontas, or Poky. Poky liked to come in the front door at great speed, especially if Columbus was sitting on the floor in a stately manner – she would dash past deliberately brushing against the old man, trying to knock him over with sheer speed. "Who, me? I was just coming in…" Columbus put up with such nonsense with grace and aplomb.

Columbus ready to travel

When Columbus was 24, he got an infection and I had to take him to the local vet, Doc Johnson, in our new Eastern Shore location. The Doc examined him, gave him some antibiotic, and asked his age. Shocked, he allowed that Cols was his oldest feline patient ever, and remarked to his assistant, "give him the Senior Citizens discount." As I left, I found out that the Senior Discount was 100% – the bill was ZERO. Columbus was to remain a patient for many more years – and was never charged a dime. Needless to say, all our other animals got taken to the same vet!

It was around this time that I first asked Cols some really important questions. (I say "asked", but this is not a verbal exchange, it is nearly always silent.)

Do you have a view of life and death, or where you and I fit in the scheme of things?
– I am more than satisfied with my current existence, but I am also sure that it is part of a whole.
But how do you see the whole? What is it, to you?
– You must learn to trust your own perspective.
I'm afraid that doesn't tell me much.
– How can I tell you more than you can understand? You are not me, I am not you. I can only tell you where to look. I can't really tell you how, except you might try to understand how very large human blinders can be.
Allright, how would I find some perspective for myself?
– Some dark night, look at the heavens.

An image popped into my head: I was bending over the coffin to kiss my mother's forehead, an impression like kissing cold marble. My mother

74

died while I was still in my teens, and my father insisted I kiss her at the viewing, before she was carted off to be changed into ashes and placed in a little plywood box and dropped into the ground – in the same grave where my father's ashes now reside. But that thing in the coffin, that cold marble, that was not my mother, my brain says.

Since that time I had buried many cats, but never really "talked" to any of them. Let alone muse with one about the meaning of life, or death. And, although Columbus and I shared many more moments of communication, it was not until he was gone – and many years later – that I finally thought about a lot more of what he had been saying to me.

In the Spring of 1993, the time finally came for us to part ways. Cols was 31 and a half. Afterwards, I sat down and wrote the following to send to my children:

Columbus
Matthews Supercat
1962-1993

I lost a good friend and long-time companion last week. He greeted me every morning and at the end of the day when I came home, sat at my side for every meal at home, was expertly underfoot whenever anything was made in the kitchen. He had become a fixture in the house, which now is terribly silent and empty.

An incredible storehouse of vitality, he nearly set a record for longevity (the record is 34). After the first twenty-five years, we used to joke every year that he would outlive all of us. He did in fact outlive most of my family. My children, now grown and gone, grew up playing with this incredible dog-chasing monster cat. My son, now 25, was convinced that this cat was immortal.

It was my misfortune to have to be the agent of his destruction. I took him to the vet -- one of the hardest things I have ever done -- and watched while they injected him and stilled his great heart.

Columbus had been having trouble with the heat wave, and had lost the use of his front left foot, probably from a stroke. He was trying to learn to walk on his elbow. Over the weekend, we were hosting two Finnish girls on their way home from a year in this country as exchange students. Cols was having more and more difficulty, so we reluctantly decided that the time had come to take him.

I was positive that the vet would immediately put him down, and when I made the appointment I said that it would probably be his last. Before we left the house, I put Cols on my chest one last time. Tears were streaming down my face; Cols saw them and stretched forward to nuzzle me repeatedly, saying, "Don't worry, it's nothing to cry about."

They saw him right away on Monday morning, and the vet said, "What can we do for you?". I put Cols on the floor and demonstrated his difficulty walking, noted his shrunken condition. "How is his appetite?" Well, actually, his appetite is just fine. He's nothing **but** a walking appetite, or a limping one. I have always been sure that, in his case, the appetite would be the last thing to go. "Well, keep on feeding him."

Well, if the professional opinion was that he was not suffering, I wasn't going to argue. Because he looked emaciated (nothing but skin and bones, his eyes had begun to shrink into his head), the vet gave me some enzyme powder to sprinkle onto his food. "This helps the digestion and works well with older cats and dogs."

I also put plastic and newspaper down on the office floor so that I could leave him in air conditioning, but Cols continued to go downhill. By Wednesday evening, he was mostly crawling. He lay on our bed, gathering strength. Then he would struggle to an upright lay-on-the-stomach position, crawl forward a few inches, and fall over on his side again.

He did not eat Wednesday night, nor again on Thursday morning. And on that last morning, he was crying, not in his normal strident FEED ME! voice, but in a weak series of meows. I brought more food to the office and he stopped crying; he just wanted to be with people. He made a half-hearted attempt to taste the food and couldn't eat it. He tried a lap or two of water and couldn't do that, either.

I could not leave him shut in a room alone, to die.

I went on to work (after I left, he cried some more for company) and called again for an appointment. I came back and took him for that last visit, 10 a.m. July 15. I picked him

up and carried him to the car. "It's the end of the road, Cols."
He lay quietly in my lap. We went into the waiting room, the
only ones there. Now he kept trying to crawl off my lap (this
is not his favorite place), so I got up and took him to the
screen door, to look outside. He watched the traffic on the
busy highway, his head swiveling.

The vet came out. "What can we do for you today." I told
him Columbus had stopped eating, it was time. "Well, let's get
if over with", he said, going to an adjacent room for his
clippers as the nurse held Cols on the table. He shaved the
inside thigh, ran a long needle into the vein. "I hate to do
this", he said. A big dose of something milky was injected,
filling the vein. Then he poked a finger in Columbus' big yellow
eye, got no reaction, poked again, and said, "He's gone." It
only took seconds.

They wanted to put him in a plastic bag and a box, but I had
brought a towel, in the car. I picked up my little furry
creature, lost my voice, mumbled something and left. I curled
him on the towel on the seat. Tears were flowing now; I
drove off blindly. Oh, Colsy-cat, Colsy-cat! Lost to me now,
forever.

I took him home and laid him on the deck while I changed into
old clothes, then dug a grave in the rock-hard ground,
parched from the heat wave and lack of rain. I picked him up
a last time, kissed the top of that familiar broad head, soft
grey fur still warm from the summer sun, placed him in the
ground still curled, covered by the towel, and then the earth.
He looks out from the banks of the Pocomoke River across
the water to the forest wilderness area, next to a trail into the
raspberry bushes made by the wild cats, my Cols cat, my
loyal and faithful beast, companion of my best years.

--Spring, 1993

Columbus in his last year

Poky's Reign

When my daughter was finishing high school, we
hosted an exchange student from Finland who also
loved animals. One day both girls went with me
when I drove our pickup to the dump with a load of
trash. Someone had dumped three tiny kittens there
to fend for themselves, and they were prancing
around the big metal drive-up containers. They
were friendly, and hungry, so naturally our girls
could not stand to leave them there. We returned
with three more cats.

Poky, the new kitten

They became happy outdoor cats on our riverbank,
and I'm sorry to say I forget two of their names (by

80

then our outdoor cattery was up to 8). The girls named them, and spoiled them, but my daughter was finding herself increasingly allergic to cats, so they stayed outside. The one whose name I remember was MaMa cat, so named because she continued to produce more litters of kittens. After a few litters, a trip to the vet put an end to the multiplication. MaMa was with us for many years, and one of her kittens, a beautiful grey, became quite close to us.

This grey with a wonderful, loving personality was Chili cat, so named because our vet likes to go to a local diner on chili day, when they have steaming bowls of their specialty, and I often would join him there for lunch. One day I told him I was naming my next cat after him, but he was surprised when I showed up for cat shots and told him the cat's name was Chili. She was an outdoor cat with lots of playmates, including Poky, but at the same time was super-friendly and would love any attention. She had ultra-soft fur.

When Chili was about a year old, she came to the front door one Spring day in very sick condition. I took her to the vet, and he was of the opinion that she was poisoned. He hydrated her but was not optimistic. Sure enough, they had just been spraying the fields, which came up close to the house. I put a towel on the living room recliner and placed her there, and nursed her, and tried to get her to take nourishment or water, but it was a lost cause and she passed away after an awful two days and nights. She joined the others on the riverbank.

A few more years went by, we visited our exchange daughter and family in Finland, our daughter got married, and we gradually lost all our outdoor cats.

At the shore, our closest friends lived just down the river. We could float there on the current when the tide was going out, or take a 5 minute walk on the road. Inside, they had a Chesapeake Retriever and a very fat cat named Mischief. Outside, they constantly had multiple cats and batches of kittens, a result of their willingness to put out plentiful food. It seemed like they were always giving away kittens, and for the most part, they found willing adopters. Three of them came to us over the years.

Poky, the world's fastest cat

The last surviving kitten of MaMa cat' second and final litter was a tiny grey and white which the neighbors said we had to call Pocohantas since we already had a Columbus. That soon became Poky for short. We also called her the "world's fastest cat", as she was often just a blur of motion. We've had experience with a **lot** of kittens, but we have never seen one before or since that came close to Poky when she was in a hurry. By the time she was half grown, no rabbit in the yard was safe. As a kitten, she loved to run more than anything. In our bedroom, she would start at one side, run to the bed and leap up, dash across the bed, run to the wall on the other side. By this time, she would have a good head of steam and would get halfway up the wall. Turning, she would repeat the performance in the other direction, going halfway up the wall on the other side. We would watch from in bed like it was a tennis match.

Poky kitten with Cols

I lay on my back in the king size bed and flung kitten Poky straight up in the air, yelling

"SWOOP!", then catching her in my hands as she came down. She loved it. Soon I modified the exclamation to "Swoop cat!". And for a long time, every time I picked her up, I would swing her towards the ceiling, my Swoop cat. Columbus and Poky were friends.

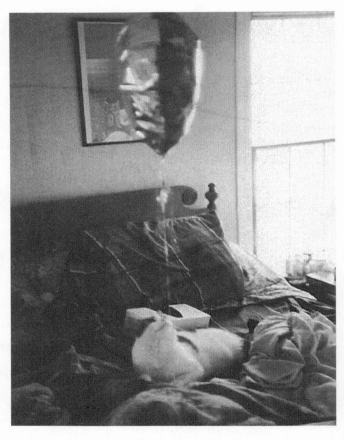

Poky loved to play with balloons, for hours

Not so with the next inside kitten that arrived. By the time J.R. came, Columbus was buried and Poky had adapted herself as the sole indoor cat, master of the domain. She turned her nose up at J.R. and raised a terrific fuss. She also developed a serious temper. When we wouldn't change the arrangements, she stayed outside in retaliation. Then she began to prefer being outside, and only came inside in the bitterest weather.

Her temper did not improve, though, and she continually got into fights with other outdoor creatures. After several years, one day I saw that she had a big scratch on her face that was swelling up. I brought her in and took her to the vet. We gave her a shot and then continued with Amoxicillin, but the infection went to her brain (wounds on the face are very close and so infection there is quite dangerous in cats). When she could no longer walk without staggering, sadly we had to put her down, and Poky was buried on the riverbank next to her longtime friend Columbus.

Let me stir up the underwear drawer, please...

Breathing Cave

For many years, we celebrated our many years with
Columbus – on Columbus Day, naturally. Our
neighbors got into the act and would arrive for the
birthday party with black armbands, decorations,
and a basket usually filled with creative gifts. One
Columbus Day we opened the basket to find a
beautiful solid grey kitten. This was Stewart, and
he grew quite large, becoming best friends with our
dog, Midge. Our neighbors on the riverbank were a
constant source of new kittens, besides keeping
many for themselves along with their Chesapeake
Retriever and two Goldens. They feed outdoor
cats, so the word spreads in the world of wild cats
and their address is a popular one.

Our neighbors always went to an annual family
reunion in McDowell, West Virginia. This always
put me in mind of the large Breathing Cave under
nearby Jack Mountain. I had spent many weeks
working in this cave over the years, personally
discovered new sections, mapped large portions of
the cave, and explored it with many friends. We
would always camp in the cave, usually for a week
or more. The room we used for camping had a nice
flat sand floor and the temperature was always in
the 50's (which feels nice and warm in winter and
nice and cool in summer). This cave has everything
– pits and crevasses, rivers and dry sections,
climbing challenges and crawlways. It also has a
cat connection...

One Winter day, I was fortunate enough to discover

an entirely new, and major, section of the cave system. In a smaller section of the cave that was seldom visited – on the "wrong" side of the entrance pitch (only a few hundred feet of passage were known on this side, whereas on the other side, through crawlway and past the sand floor room, there was a major cave system), I fought my way up a slippery mud wall that sloped backwards, to get a look at the top, and, YES! there was a small passageway up there. This in turn led to some large passages and eventually came out overlooking a large crevasse, at least 60 feet down to the bottom.

No problem rappelling down, I had plenty of rope with me, but coming back up presented more difficulty. I've never been a fan of climbing a rope with prussik knots or their mechanical brethren. It's slow and laborious at best, and nasty when the rope hangs against a wall or crevasse side (not so bad if the rope hangs in midair). So I measured with rope and then went back for 60 feet of cable ladder (we always carried several 30 foot lengths on explorations, and they were stored in the camping room). Just as it sounds, this is two lengths of stainless steel aircraft cable. About every 18 inches were placed hollow aluminum rungs, held top and bottom with rivets on the cables. A 30 foot length rolls up to about a foot in diameter and can clip to your backpack. They are very lightweight, strong, and easy to climb.

I returned with the ladders and several more friends eager to see virgin cave territory including a major crevasse passage that extended as far as our lights would reach in both directions. We secured a rappelling rope and the cable ladder to a large rock and rappelled down into the crevasse; as discoverer, I had the honor to go first. The crevasse floor was quite flat and varied in width from about ten to twenty feet. But what awaited us, and astounded me right away, was another most amazing discovery.

All along the walls on both sides – wherever it was mud covered and not just rock – were hundreds and hundreds of large claw marks. Obviously, something got stuck in here in the dark and tried to climb out, perhaps came in a small entrance on the mountainside, took a nap and got lost, or the entrance caved in. It was truly eerie looking at these big marks – and I mean big, like a maybe a bear? – no, we decided, it had to be a mountain lion or some kind of large cat. Was it still in here?

I tell you, that is a funny feeling. There was no way to tell how fresh or how old these marks were. They could have been made yesterday, or they could be a hundred years old. There was nothing in the cave system that would disturb them. I took my camera out of my backpack and took a bunch of pictures (yes, I still have them). I put a quarter up next to one of the deepest scratches down the wall to show the scale – a mark about four inches wide and six or seven inches long. The size mark you could make with a man's hand, except that it wouldn't have the sharp claws at the tips.

The passage went on for many hundreds of feet, and so did the claw marks. The direction of the passage would take it to the side of the mountain in one direction, so we theorized that there could be a small entrance somewhere there. There was a small intersecting passage in one spot about three or four feet off the floor – just a hole, but shining a light in it I could see that there was a passable crawlway. No caver could pass up something like that, it might lead to even more sections of virgin cave. So I crawled in. There was just barely room to crawl along the hard mud floor.

Now, this is also a strange sensation, to be crawling in a one-way tube with the knowledge that there could be something with very large claws up ahead. All was silence except for the hissing of the carbide light on my helmet. Finally, after what seemed like 100 feet and was probably 30, I came to the end. The tube widened into a perfectly round small room, also covered with claw marks. Our friend had tried to get out this way, too!

We never did find any other evidence – no skeletons or carcasses or fur. To my knowledge, the mystery of the Breathing Cave claw marks has never been definitively settled. But they are there, they are huge, and **something** made them sometime.

A very small section of the Breathing Cave clawmarks

Oliver

A distant cousin came to visit, after announcing that he was moving to a distant state and asking if he could "temporarily" house his cat with us. It turned out that his new apartment did not allow cats, so the temporary part became permanent, and at that point we gave Oliver to my son, who needed a new cat. But before that took place, we had Oliver in our little house on the riverbank for the better part of a year.

Oliver was a huge cat, at least twenty pounds, a neutered male tiger who was totally spoiled and had always been an indoor-only cat. After a month or so, we decided it was time to introduce him to the outdoor world. After all, the weather was nice and our driveway was more than 700 feet long, so there was little danger of accident from road traffic. We let him out to discover the adjacent riverbank and the rest of nature's creatures. He slunk away, his large belly an inch from the ground, scared out of his mind.

At the end of the day, there was no sign of Oliver, so I had to go searching. Calling him got no response, so I widened my search pattern. Finally found him hiding in my neighbor's barn. Dragged him back to the house. Next day, same thing. At least I knew where to look this time. After about a week of this Oliver started to actually observe some of the outside world that he could see through a small barn door.

Soon Oliver loved the outdoors and didn't want to be anywhere else. And he discovered that he could own the place, as nothing would stand up to him – he was just too big. One day when Oliver was inside we made the mistake of leaving the front door open so that cooling Spring breezes could come through the screen door. They weren't the only thing coming through the screen door – Oliver wanted out, so he just marched right through the screen!

We had a screened-in deck on the river side of the house, and before you know it, Oliver was teaching the other cats – including heretofore strictly outdoor cats – how to come up onto the deck where the cat food was stored. Screens? No problem, just add a little more steam and walk right in! Actually, Oliver made such a big hole that the others didn't have to do anything but follow. But they learned, too, because after Oliver went to my son's house, they continued the practice and I had to install decorative gratings over the screens they could reach.

All went well at my son's house, with Oliver spending a great deal of his time outside lording it over the neighborhood, and coaxing extra meals out of the neighbors. Then, of course, one night he was out and wanted in. So he found a window with a screen...

Never met a screen that stood in the way. So they had to leave one small bedroom window cracked open and sporting a permanent torn screen.

Oliver

One evening they wished they had gotten a video
camera out, because they would have had a
wonderful submission to America's funniest
videos. They brought home fast food, and one of the

bags contained crumbs from nachos with cheese. They put it on the floor, and Oliver promptly dove into it, headfirst. Next thing they knew, the bag was being propelled all over the floor as Oliver frantically scrambled with his front paws to get deeper and deeper into the bag. Picture a taco bag zipping all around with the tail end of a very large cat protruding, blindly running into furniture and walls...

One day, as cats will do, Oliver went out and did not return. This mystery was solved the following Spring when a very large cat skeleton was discovered under the bushes at the side of the house. Was he poisoned? Did he meet an even larger creature? We'll never know. But one thing is sure, Oliver grew to love life and the outdoors and his personality was as massive as his great body.

Harry

Once in a rare while, a creature comes into your life with extraordinary capabilities and capacities, throws himself into everything with huge, unstoppable zest. Combined with outstanding intellect, that was Harry.

A neighborhood stray adopted my son and kept coming into their house. "Not my cat", Kevin said, since he already had several other cats. "I think the cat has different ideas", I said. When their family named the cat Delilah, I knew they were sunk. Shortly thereafter Delilah camped under Kevin's desk and produced kittens. Six weeks later I decided that one of these kittens would be a great birthday present for my wife, as well as a re-vitalizing tonic for our two older, set-in-their-ways cats.

She didn't quite see it that way. "Not my idea," she said. "I don't want another cat, don't want a kitten, I'm allergic to cats." "You can take the kitten," she went on, "but it's NOT MY CAT, period." So at the end of her birthday celebration, we loaded the kitten into the car and drove the 30 miles home. During the trip, kitten managed to disappear multiple times and was coaxed from some unknown hiding spot after we were home, thereupon being christened "Harry Houdini" for his vanishing acts.

Small enough to fit in the palm of your hand, Harry was deep black with a white chest, white gloves on all four feet and tip of tail. He looked like a

Sylvester and reminded me of a miniature Penguin. And, of course, he was all mischief. The older cats immediately announced their displeasure in no-uncertain hisses and growls, which Harry ignored as being below his notice. Cute as a button, he would play with anything and everything.

Harry has arrived

Within a matter of weeks, Harry had displaced the older cats from all their usual resting places, including the bed. He insisted on sleeping on top of Mom. Mom would throw him off, literally making him airborne. He thought that a great game and would march right back. "Great fun, Mom, do it again!" Eventually she gave up and Harry settled down for the night. After a few nights, she completely surrendered to the superior persistence. It probably didn't hurt that he would crawl up as far as possible and tilt his head way back in order to give her the most adoring looks she has ever received from any beast, including me (this was a habit he never gave up). I took great pleasure in reminding Mom about "her" cat, as there was no question whose cat this was. Not that we weren't pals – I just didn't get the adoring looks.

He was perfectly happy to play with me, though. And in a couple more weeks he perfected the ambush of each of the other cats, leaping upon them and trying to see just how much of the back of their necks he could get into his mouth. The fact that he was one quarter their size made no difference whatsoever. Harry gave no quarter and expected none. When they tired of the game and struck back, he would retreat a barely safe distance and start over. Again, persistence ruled the day. Eventually we had to make clear to him that only so much attacking of the others would be appreciated. They weren't quite up to his love of play.

Harry started talking early. Most of the cats of my acquaintance don't talk much – maybe 20% will occasionally speak, mostly to get attention, and maybe 10% are really talkative. Harry was in the latter category, announcing his conquests, demanding response, but mostly just saying, "It's me! I did it!". Throw a toy and he would cry out, then go fetch it, announce again that he had it, then bring it back, with or without teaching it a lesson first. But he only talked to humans, never to the other cats. He would also greet complete strangers, again only the human kind. He got an early start on learning English, too. I've had only one other cat who build an impressive vocabulary – even learned to spell, God's honest truth – but you already know about Columbus.

Harry quickly learned his name, and by the time he was six months old, he also understood "Get Down!", "Leave Zoe alone!", "That's not yours!", "Fetch!", "beast", and "birgie" (a feathered toy, as in "Go get your Birgie!").

Our cats have automatic feeders and waterers, but they do sometimes run out if we aren't paying attention. J.R., the old man, will come get me if this is the case, but Harry also quickly proved adept at the same errand and before long became the first to announce our shameful lack in the refill department. When less than half grown, he soon proved adept at all the things the other cats could do, and he began to add other accomplishments. Observing that the other cats could climb where they thought he could not reach, he soon taught them additional ways to get to the high places and found some nooks that he thought they should learn. Still a kitten, he began to surpass Zoe, our best hunter, in the catching of mice. To play with, of course.

Almost any cat can learn to use a litter box, and it was no surprise that Harry could adapt when tiny, as we moved his box from bedroom to upstairs hall, then finally to distant downstairs laundry room. And he caught on to the other cats going outside for the purpose. Our cats also have to learn some special door behavior. Our weaving studio has a cat door to the outside, but to use it you (the cat) must wear a special magnet on your collar (otherwise the raccoons get in, ask me how we know!). You also must learn to turn your head just so, to allow the magnet to tell the catch to release and let the door open. It took our current cats two days to learn this trick; it took Harry 28 minutes. Of course, he had the advantage of following them. Some days all three in a row would go in and out, in and out, for an hour or more, just for sport.

We also had several inside doors that are spring-loaded and close themselves, to keep heat or air conditioning within zones. As anyone who has owned cats knows, if you bar a cat from entry into a specific room, that is the only room the cat wants to be in. And after you let them in, the only thing they want is to go out again. Our older cats are adept at opening these doors in both directions, and of course Harry caught on immediately. He then invented the game of making a circular journey through the rooms, banging through two sets of doors, preferably chasing either one or two other cats for sport until they would get tired and give up the chase.

"I'm ready to play!"

When my wife came home from a stay in the
hospital, we installed a heater in the bathroom and
set it to keep the bath warmer than the rest of the
floor. Of course, we had to keep the door closed
for this to work. Unfortunately, Harry would open
the door and leave it open, so we had to install a
spring on this door as well. This new spring was
much stronger than the ones on the other doors, and
the cats could not get it open (my wife complained
that it was even hard for **her** to operate). But Harry
had formed the habit of coming in the bathroom
every morning when I went in, and then jumping up
and walking back and forth on the edge of the sink
and rubbing on me. The new strong spring stymied
him for exactly one day. On the second morning of
the new spring, he backed up across the hall, gave
a running start, and slammed into the door with his
shoulder, gaining entrance proudly. The other cats,

twice his size, still didn't get in, and they were also regular morning bath visitors.

In our family, Harry's biggest fame is in woobie retrieval. Yes, I know, that takes a bit of explaining. As even the tiniest kitten, Harry loved toys. One of the things I found around the house was an old toy consisting of a fake raccoon tail (with two beady eyes) attached to a plastic ball. Inside the ball was a motor and two batteries so that the ball would roll around and drag the tail. It usually scares dogs and cats silly, they can't wait to run away from this thing. Harry, of course, pounced on it even though it was bigger than he was.

After a couple of weeks of chasing this around, the motor quit and could not be convinced to run again. So I cut the raccoon tail with eyeballs off and tossed it across the room. "WOW!", said Harry, bounding after it. He grabbed it. "YOW!", he said, "I got it!". Then he brought it back to me to throw again. "What are you," I said, "a dog?" "You want to play fetch?" "YOW!".
"All right," I said, throwing it again, "fetch!". It immediately became his favorite toy of all time, and fetch became his favorite game.

If he was bored, I could say, "Go get your beast!", and he would find his toy and bring it back, carrying it in his mouth and leaping up on the bed with an announcement, "YOW!". "You've got your beast!" "YOW!".

Shortly thereafter, my wife observed that Harry would bring the captured toy to his nap and cradle it in his paws. "Look," she said, "he wants to sleep with his woobie." And so it became a woobie, and although it was carried around a lot, it was never far from Harry and he could always find it. In fact, he could find it on command. Harry would come in the bedroom looking bored. "Go get your beast", I said – for I always referred to it that way, "Ah, you've got your beast!". And he would go get it, teach it a lesson, and bring it to bed.

After some weeks of this, the woobie began to appear a bit dusty, as you might imagine. Not sure if it could actually be laundered, I looked in stores for some new toys. Briefly, a group of bird-things – kind of like badminton birds, little throwable things with feathers – were popular for fetching, but Harry always returned to the woobie. Catnip-filled pillows with mouse pictures? Forget it! Stuffed mice toys? Strings? Nope. Woobie only, please.

Harry with his woobie

Of course, my hand under the covers, or my fingers poking out, would also be a favorite thing to attack. He was fearless. I could raise my hand up, inside the covers, until it towered over him. He would crouch a bit, then spring up and pounce on top of my hand, wrestling it down with both front legs wrapped around and mouth engaged with the biggest bite he could get. When it was time to settle, he would sleep on top of Mom for a bit, then later come over and curl up to lean on my side for the rest of the night.

As Harry grew to nine months, his coat grew sleek and glossy, his legs grew long, and when he sat up tall with the black magnet in the center of his white vest just like a bow tie, he looked just like a cat in a tux. His fur was wonderfully soft and his tail was full, here was the very picture of the young cat at perfect health.

Harry reminded us of our most famous cat, Columbus, in another way. He found that he could climb a tree behind the house and jump down onto the roof of an addition visible outside my office window. Just to prowl, looking for trouble. We could also see him from the bedroom, peering over the edge at the ground below. Then he discovered that he could climb the posts supporting the little roof over the front door. This roof projects over a front deck and actually overhangs the supporting posts, so there is no way down. Fearless Harry just jumped one full floor down to the wooden deck.

Things began to get strange when my wife, with no real warning, had a heart attack and was taken to the emergency room by ambulance. Next thing I knew, I was practically camped at the hospital and then she was undergoing open heart surgery, a quadruple bypass, valve repair, and so on. Sixteen days later she was able to come home, but faced a long road of recovery.

Neighbors were leaving food, and I was scrambling up and down while Mom stayed in our bedroom on the second floor. The day after she came home, I failed to put away cheese sauce leftovers on the kitchen counter, and I saw the next morning that you-know-who got into it.

Meantime, Harry had to be trained not to get on top of Mom's incision, but he soon learned to curl up lower on her body. He continued to come as close as he could to give those looks of love.

A week after Mom had come home from the hospital, overnight Harry was not curled at my side, and when I got up in the middle of the night for my bathroom run, I had to step over him spread out on my office floor. I thought it a bit strange but didn't pay that much attention. In the morning, he was stretched out on the floor of the upstairs hallway, and had no interest in opening the bathroom door. Now I picked him up, and he was obviously in great pain.

I called the vet, and they scheduled an appointment for 3:30 p.m. My first thought was that he was blocked up with that cheese sauce, but I had seen both he and our older cat, J.R., digging in the front lawn on Monday morning. He was in pain all day, and the vet could find no sign of poisoning or infection or any kind of fight – normal temperature, no marks or bleeding, nothing. "I think he's been hit", said the vet. I thought that would be very strange, because our driveway is 700 feet long and Harry had never ventured to the road. Also, he had a healthy respect for cars, always dashing away when we started one.

Anyway, nothing was broken, so the vet gave him a shot of penicillin and 200ml of saline intramuscularly and said to call him in the morning. I took him home, brought him to the bedroom and made him as comfortable as possible. He continued to howl periodically. Sadly, he also continued downhill. I felt helpless as his body grew colder and his eyes glazed and I guess he slipped into a coma. We went to bed and at 10:45 p.m. I heard him make a noise. I got up and turned on a light and saw that he had completely turned over and was gone. I tried to massage some life back into his body, now completely relaxed and soft, but he had left us.

In the morning, we both cried. I buried him on the riverbank, next to Poky and Columbus, with his furry "woobie" in his paws.

It took a week for us to figure out what had happened. We both remembered hearing a huge "thump" in the middle of the night – so loud that my wife had me get up to see if someone had come in the driveway (they hadn't). There had been no more of these sounds after Harry was gone. Then we remembered that there had been previous "thumps" in the night, not quite as loud. In a flash we realized that it was Harry jumping from the front roof to the deck in front of the cat door. On this last occasion – Monday night – he must have hit the railing or something, then staggered through the cat door and upstairs. But obviously he had sustained internal injuries and they killed him in one day. Later I figured it out when I found that a spatula had fallen off the barbeque, gone through a crack in the deck floorboards and landed with the narrow handle pointing up. Just about where a jumping cat could land on it.

Perhaps he was a little too fearless, but his joy and spirit reminded me of many other young males, thousands of which plunge into dangerous activities every year feeling immortal. Some of these seriously injure or kill themselves, so I guess it is a standard practice of nature. It doesn't make it any easier to lose him, but at least we don't feel it is our fault.

We continue to celebrate the way he lived, blazing like a meteor, a life brief but incandescent. Some of the outstanding cats I have known I have been able to learn from, as their approach to life – whether to problems or just to the art of living itself – is usually simple, direct, and profound. We tend to make things complicated, intellectualizing and rationalizing everything that happens. What Harry taught me was not only to "seize the day", but also to appreciate its worth. And he made me realize that I should tell his story along with some others.

J.R.'s Tale

Only a few days have passed since J.R. left us, making this very difficult to write as I sit here looking at his picture. He had a very unique and memorable face; I knew it as well as any in my life, and he knew mine as well. In fact, his face was somewhat famous.

When he was quite young, we had a business doing pet portraits, mostly at dog and cat shows in the mid-Atlantic. In 1999 I had developed a process for making digital paintings from photos. On July 27, 2000 I took a photo of a 16-month-old J.R. reposing in the bathroom sink (it was a hot day); his expression gave vent to the photo caption: "Get Your Own Sink!". And in 2001 I made this photo into a painting. It was subsequently made into prints on canvas and paper, on notecards, and even printed on silk scarves, and sold to many animal lovers. It's still popular today, more than a decade later. His face never really changed with age, but it has gotten hard for me to look at the picture.

The famous Digi-Art image of J.R.

As I told him the day before he left us, we had some good times. But finally a disease came that we could not control, and his last night he spent cuddled under the covers with me, both of us unable to sleep. Taking him the next morning for euthanasia was a job I have always hated. I don't like the idea of playing God with a creature's life. Certainly this has to be one of the hardest tasks in my life; guilt and sadness are the immediate result. But I steeled myself and rubbed his neck as he was put away, then brought him back home and buried him at the edge of the woods in his favorite spot for daily watching. In his last year, he could be seen every day from the kitchen window, watching the world. It's difficult to look at that spot now, we expect to see him there. At my age and state of health, there is little doubt that he was the last cat whose whole normal life I will attend.

"Friends" – J.R. and George, constant companions

111

Can killing, the stopping of a valued existence, be excused in the name of love? And if not, is it more excusable to stand idly by and watch the suffering? The answer is obvious but no less difficult. In the end, justifying the act is not really important except to gird us to our responsibility. We know also that we are sentencing ourselves to grief and regret over the loss of our faithful companion. I do not believe that we will meet again or exist again; the past is past and will not repeat (and as we age, it increases in value). The sense of love is all that remains of our joy. Would that I could bring it back.

J.R.'s last month was difficult, with difficulty urinating and the result mostly blood. A week of antibiotics failed and analysis showed the type of cells common in bladder cancers. He had major breathing troubles and at 12.5 years of age was down to 5 pounds; no further treatment was possible. He had begun to look for places to hide from the pain, and on the last day finally stopped eating. Looking back farther than that last month, for most of his life he had major health problems. And yet, and yet…until this one, he mastered them all.

J.R. came into the world just before the new century. He lived at our neighbors in a box outside with his litter mates and something came along and chewed his front paws to hamburger. The neighbor brought him inside, let him heal, and put him with the outside cats again. It happened a second time, and she brought him in and let him heal again. They

112

called him "Tiny Tim" – he bravely soldiered on. The third time it happened, she said she guessed they would have to put him down, and we volunteered to take him instead.

He healed once again, and soon was at home in our house, despite Poky's objections. His second name became "Stumpy", due to the crashing thuds coming down the stairs as a club footed kitten. He was ready to take life in big bites. At some point we started to call him "Junior" since he was much smaller (and younger) than our other cats, and this was eventually shortened to J.R. He had to have surgery on his front paws, and have a couple of ingrown claws removed, but never showed any sign of slowing down – on the contrary, as regards the other cats, both indoor and outdoor, his attitude was "anything you can do, I can do better!".

Poky decided that she could not bear to live in a house with another cat; she took it as a great insult that we would bring in another, even though she had lived with Columbus in the house. She spent more and more time outside, and eventually decided she would rather stay out, and eat out. She grew to love the riverbank with its many creatures, and only came in, reluctantly, on the coldest nights. J. R. was completely unfazed whether Poky was in or out, hissing or not. To J. R., another cat was just immaterial. If there was another cat on the bed, J. R. would sleep on the bed also; if the other cat wanted to sleep separately, that was OK, too.

When J. R. was just about grown, we heard about a

cat door that could be installed, and bought one at our local hardware superstore. After all, we had the perfect location for one – our 700 foot driveway was nowhere near the road, our cats were allowed to go out whenever they wanted, and it would be great if they could come in while we were away, whenever they needed to. So we installed the door in our studio, in the door that went to the front deck.

Everything went swimmingly until our dog died. We didn't think anything about it until we went away for a weekend. When we returned, there was a big mess in the dining room and pantry, food scattered everywhere. We assumed that one or more of the outdoor wild cats had gotten in and made a mess. We went away for another weekend, and this time the mess was really terrific, including leaving the freezer door open, scattered previously-frozen chicken breasts on the floor, etc., etc. What could have opened the standup freezer door? Surely not a cat. The culprit had also spilled a 5 pound container of cocoa, and left tracks. Mr. Raccoon!

There are lots of raccoons on the riverbank, they use it as a superhighway. When we had a dog, they did not come near. But obviously they had put a sign on the riverbank, "Dog dead, party at the Matthews". And, of course, they had observed the use of the cat door and did the same.

Before we could do anything about this, the very next night I awoke to loud growling downstairs. I went down and turned on the studio lights. There was J. R., standing his ground and growling at a large raccoon in the studio. The raccoon looked up at me. I said, "Out! Out!". He slowly turned around and ambled leisurely to the cat door and through it. It looked to me like he was three times the size of the door opening, but he slipped out like it was a perfect fit.

The following day I did some serious research. There was a product made from coyote urine which repels raccoons (they are a favorite coyote meal, so are very chary of being anywhere there might be coyotes). That should work, since the dog worked. But a very expensive product. Then I discovered that the newer models of the cat door worked on a magnet. If the cats wore a magnet on the collar, the door would work. No magnet, no door operation. Worked like a charm – never had another problem. Ever since, we have always had a magnetic cat door and our cats have been deliriously happy to go in and out at all hours of their pleasure (except when they tangle with something and lose the collar and magnet).

J. R. might not have tolerated raccoons, but he was perfectly happy to share with other cats. He was friendly to Poky, even though this was not reciprocated. And he was happy to share bed and food with Zoe, and with Harry. After Zoe was gone and Harry met his untimely end, we brought in George to be Mom's cat, and J. R. was happy to play with the new kitten; in fact, it reinvigorated him and he connected with his childhood. They would take turns chasing each other through the house at top speed.

J.R.'s biggest challenge started when he was about 2. He developed a serious case of chronic Rhinitis, snorting and slurping all through the day. His nose leaked constantly, and at the worst times his lungs bled. He was forced to breathe through his mouth, and learned that breathing was easiest when he was washing something (consequently, our other cats, furniture, etc. were constantly bathed). His first symptoms quickly turned to pneumonia, but fortunately a course of Amoxicillin battled this back to just congestion and leakage. This condition remained with him the rest of his life – I took to calling him "my snortcat". Rhinitis is fairly common in cats and is supposed to be highly infectious to other cats who have the susceptibility, but none of our other cats ever contracted it. J.R. would go along for a month or two, then develop pneumonia on top of the Rhinitis. Eventually the vet provided me with a stock of Amoxicillin so we could be prepared. I lost count of the number of times we had to mix a new batch. J.R. refused to be inconvenienced, he compensated for not being able to breathe and carried on.

This went on for many years. We used to predict that he would not "live through another winter", but he proved us wrong so many times that we stopped making dire predictions. He absolutely met every challenge in his life with amazing bravery. Toward the end of his life he began to look very bad – he was down to a skeleton with fur, and very ratty, mangy fur at that. But at the same time he was a jealous guard of the cat food with plenty of appetite. When I checked with vet suggestions online, one of them said, "if not doing well, give them chicken soup – it's what Mom gave me!". I tried it, and sure enough, there was great improvement.

He could not breathe through his nose and had to keep his mouth open. Usually his tongue was sticking out as he slurped his way through the day. You always knew when he was in the room.

Eventually we decided to change his diet, and took him off the commercial dry cat food. We put him on a "carnivore" diet – dry cat food with no grain, plus some canned cat food also grain-free. Then we supplemented with a quarter-teaspoon of L. Lysine powder. He bulked right up and his coat became beautiful again; the change was amazing.

After this, J.R. was in the best of health (though still snorting) for the last year of his life until the final month. He garnered still another name when he began the habit of sitting on the foot of our bed every morning and loudly demanding breakfast – we called him "the alarm cat". For most of his life I did not communicate with him as with Columbus, but nevertheless we had a close non-verbal understanding.

For the last several years of his life, J.R. and George became the closest of companions, washing each other every day. Mostly this habit grew out of

J.R.'s difficulty breathing; he discovered it was easier if he continually "snorted" and if he licked everything in sight – bed frame, furniture, people, other cats. We grew accustomed to constant "slurp, slurp" sounds in the house whenever he was awake. Eventually George decided she might as well take advantage of the free baths. We knew if we went away to a show on a weekend that they would take good care of each other, and worried that after J.R. passed that George would need a companion.

In the last two years of his life, a remarkable thing happened. J.R., sitting on the arm of my recliner and gazing at me, began to communicate! I had assumed up to that time that Columbus was the one remarkable communicator it had been my destiny to know, and at first I assumed that my own mind was making up the interaction with J.R. based on my previous experiences with Cols. But gradually I learned that it was I who had to learn the right way, and as a result I was able to have many exchanges with J.R. before he left us.

I never told anyone about this; I assumed that someday I might tell Columbus' story but thought that if I added J.R. everyone would assume I was somewhat batty. I suppose this is still the case, but I no longer care. I remember one of our latter exchanges:

What are you thinking when you look at my face?
– That I will always know you.
And I you, whenever or wherever we meet. We are

bonded.

– Yes

Were you aware that Cols and I talked like this?

– Anyone can do it if they know how to listen

How will we bond after life?

– I do not look ahead; I live a simple life in the now

But is our bond forever?

– Lacking claws and sharp teeth, humans have expanded brains. It is both a blessing and a curse. You overprocess everything. I don't use my brain the way you do. Love, in the here and now, is enough.

But for me, I want more. I don't want Cols and J.R. to be gone forever. Now that they are gone, I've listened for echoes in the quiet night, but have not found them. I'd like to think that when I die, I will be with my family and Cols and J.R. and all the rest in the big unity. Or perhaps we will just start over, and maybe my favorite friends have already done so somewhere. Or, the most bittersweet, that there is only the one reality.

It was a sad time when it became necessary to let go. J.R. is a part of history now, he joins Zoe and Harry and Poky and Chili and Cols and Nan and Gabe and the rest, a long unbroken line much loved. I commend his face to you, a direct vision of love.

I know J.R.'s face, and he knows mine.

Zoe's Tale

The only failure I ever had in getting along with an adopted cat was a Bengal named Hindu, or as we called her, Nefertiti. I always wanted a Bengal. In my capacity as a pet portrait artist (an occupation I took up after retirement, with some success), I had occasion to go to a cat show now and then, and was always fascinated by these Bengals, looking exactly like a miniature version of their namesake. Absolutely gorgeous creatures! But they cost upwards of a thousand dollars in the early 1990's, too rich for my blood.

In those days as I was about to retire from my eighth or ninth career (this one supporting computers for the U.S. Navy), I joined a local barbershop chorus. I thoroughly enjoyed this group, served as President of the local chapter for four different years, and had great fun MC'ing their shows. During the years I was active, I sang Baritone, Bass, and Tenor parts, and helped form a registered quartet, The Last Chord, where I sang Bass. Recently I had the fun of participating in a reunion of the quartet (we are now separated by a thousand miles), and it seemed as if we could pick right up where we left off.

One day a singer in my chorus asked if anyone wanted a Bengal cat, for free. It seemed his grandaughter was moving to a new apartment (and a new boyfriend, allergic to cats). I jumped. In a week or two, arrangements were made and Hindu was delivered to us. "If it doesn't work out," said the grandaughter, "ring me up in New Jersey and I'll work something else out. This cat and I are very much kindred souls, and we're both particular about who we get along with. Oh, and Hindu comes with a companion, my tortoiseshell, Zoe," she said, handing over a strikingly handsome full grown tortoiseshell cat, who ran upstairs and hid under the nearest bed.

WOW! So we were proud owners of a gen-u-ine Bengal! A very gorgeous feline, but we were unprepared for the amount of **noise** generated by a Bengal, or at least **this** Bengal. A horrendous caterwauling filled the house, driving the other cats far away. Maybe it wants special food – or special attention – or – but no matter what we did, the offensively loud howls continued.

This can't be right. The cat is pronounced well by the vet and has had all her shots. I've had cats all my life and all have responded to love and attention and food. Granted, some are more picky than others. And some must have **their** bed, or box, or corner, etc. Nefertiti (re-named by me) came with her own cage and we were told that she preferred to live in it. But no matter whether she was free to roam, given a bed or her cage, or tempted with gourmet food, she sounded like the unhappiest cat in three counties (and I think all three counties could hear her).

Nefertiti

Finally in desperation we moved Nefertiti and her cage, with food and water, to the screened-in porch and started efforts to contact her previous owner. "Maybe she just can't live with anyone else," I told my wife. "After all, she did say they were a lot alike." Fortunately, it was late summer and temperatures were mild. Meantime, Midge, our outside dog, and her cat companion Stewart – who had been enjoying their own access to the porch through a pet door – took off for parts unknown. And did not come back to be fed. The house still filled with howls, the decibels only lightly tamed by shut doors.

Eventually the previous owner reappeared to get Nefer– uh, Hindu, and Zoe scurried upstairs to hide. We brought out Bengal and cage, and were informed that the boyfriend problem had been solved. Not sure if that meant the boyfriend was gone, or the allergy. "And how is Zoe doing?". So my wife went upstairs and came down with Zoe in her arms. Zoe took one look at her former owner and leaped for safety, sprinting back up the stairs. "She never did like me very much," said the owner. We assured her that Zoe was welcome to stay with us. I'm not sure whether it was the owner that Zoe disliked, or the howler. Or both.

Amazingly – and this is God's honest truth – within an hour after the departure of Hindu, Midge and Stewart reappeared on the porch after being missing for weeks. Both gave me looks that clearly said "Thank GOD you got rid of it." Or maybe it was "What took you so long?" Zoe came down and curled up on the couch. The other cats magically came forth. Harmony re-ensued.

We later learned, from a friend in the pet business, that Bengals are only a few years removed from the wild, and are notoriously hard to keep. "Many professionals will not deal with them," we were advised. Live and learn.

On the other hand, Zoe was a joy to have as an addition to the family. She took to everyone right away, immediately learned to use the cat door and to boss J.R. around (he loved it). But she was easygoing, ate whatever food was around without complaint, never bothered anyone, and only insisted on one thing – her loving. She was a very loving cat, and would come to each of us once a day to demand the attention – if necessary, placing her head under your hand. "Scary eyes," said my wife, "especially at night." But I didn't think so; they were bright Citrine yellow and went well with her very dark complexion and orange highlights.

J.R., now getting toward middle age, started following Zoe around. Everywhere. If Zoe went out, J.R. was right behind. If, in frustration, Zoe came right back in, so did J.R. When in a playful mood, they would dash through the upstairs rooms, switching off as to who was leading and who was following. Our doors to the upstairs hallway remain closed, but the cats know how to open them with a push. They made a circuit – bedroom to studio to hall to office to bedroom, around and around, faster and faster! It certainly gave J.R. his exercise.

Zoe

Eventually Zoe learned that there were places she could go where J.R. was unlikely to follow. She could hunt on the animal trails along the riverbank, and he would not. She could curl up for hours as a paperweight on my desk – he might come up and stay with her briefly, but would rarely stay. On the other hand, J.R. would regularly walk the narrow windowsills of the bedroom (originally a sunroom, it is all windows overlooking our wilderness river), and she would not.

They became not only companions, but best friends, much to the disgust of Poky, who had been displaced by J.R. (at least in her own mind) and remained an outside cat by her own choosing, so as not to have to truck with these upstarts. Midge and Stewart remained the closest of companions and also preferred to stay outside, even when invited to come in from the most awful weather conditions. They would, however, curl up together with a blanket on the porch.

After several years of indoor tranquility, we got a new kitten – Harry – and a year later, another new kitten, Georgy Girl. But shortly before Georgy came on the scene, Zoe suddenly lost a lot of weight. She went in a few weeks from a solid, healthy cat to skin and bones. But she continued to eat and had no other symptoms. The vet could find nothing wrong. But J.R. had encountered a similar problem about 8 months before. On the advice of a friend with an aging cat, I fed J.R. a nutritional milk supplement, first for twice a day, and as he improved, once a day, and finally tapered off completely after he had regained his weight in about six months. The vet agreed that this could help Zoe, but it had no effect and she continued to go downhill.

After some weeks with dietary supplements, she became lethargic and started showing signs I knew all too well. Sadly, I took her back to the vet, fully expecting him to put her to sleep. Instead, he gave her an antibiotic and injected about 200cc of saline under the skin to try to re-hydrate her. She figeted and did not want the saline. As I was putting her back in the crate, she suddenly stiffened and died. My son later told me it was fluid shock.

I think she was only about 7 or 8 years old. She had to have some major systemic failure to go from very healthy cat to death's door in a matter of weeks. On our last visit to the vet, she was obviously dying. We both wish we could have identified the cause.

Bengals may be striking and dramatic, but no more handsome cat ever graced our household than our beloved Zoe. I buried Zoe on the riverbank with the other cats, and we miss her. J.R. was mystified as to the sudden loss of his constant companion. He continued to hiss at the new kitten and ignore it, but it would not be long before he would find room in his heart for another.

Zoe and I were able to communicate to a minor degree. She was an equal opportunity cat, just as happy to be on my lap as Mom's. She had a lot of affection and did not need to be encouraged to jump up and be petted; it was most frequently **her** idea. One of these occasions went like this:

You are a beautiful and loving cat.
– And you are mine, always
And you are very happy here.

– I need no other family, this is perfect.
Will you help J. R.? He has trouble breathing
– He and I are fine together.

Stewart & Midge

It was just after Thanksgiving and very cold. I drove past the edge of the woods on my way north, and eight or ten puppies scampered across the road in front of me and into the ditch and then the woods. It was getting dark and I couldn't see much more, but made a mental note to check the area. Next day I drove to the site, about a half mile from home, and there were a whole bunch of very young, cold and hungry puppies, obviously abandoned in the country.

A few days later, after checking with any neighbor who could possibly own this batch and finding no one with any knowledge of the pups, I found that 5 of them had meandered down to our property on the river. I called my son and he came down and helped to round them up. Checking the site where I had first seen them, we found no more. The vet confirmed that they were not more than 6 or 8 weeks old.

Two more friends came and selected a puppy, and my son took one for his family and one for a friend. To get his, my son had to scale the riverbank to the south where it was wild and overgrown next to an adjacent field, and carry it back from the water's edge. This dog, named Rescue, was a steady companion to his family for many years until, deaf as a post, it was struck by a car from the rear and then abandoned in a hit-and-run. We took the last one left, the runt of the litter (no more than half the size of the others), and named her Midge (Midget).

130

It had been several years since we had lived with a
fuzzy little puppy; we had almost forgotten about
chewing on shoes and tearing up things. But Midge
was really a delight and anxious to please. She
loved games, especially playing catch, and ignored
the cats. Our last dog before this one was a black
Lab, and Midge, a Heinz 57 variety with longish
curly brown hair, would grow to about the same
size. At the same time, our river neighbors about
half a mile away had another kitten that needed a
home, a robust grey who already had a name:
Stewart. We brought him home, of course.
So Stewart and Midge instantly bonded, and grew
up together. They slept together, ate together,
played together, went on walks together, and
guarded the property when we were out. It was
amusing to see them take up positions as we left the

131

driveway, and see them awaiting us on our return. Midge would also announce the arrival of any car in the driveway, her bark coming long before we would be aware of any visitors. Stewart, for his part, was not interested in any cat activities that did not involve his close friend. I'm still not sure if Stewart thought he was a dog or if Midge thought she was a cat, but in any case they were inseparable.

As these two grew to full size, they became even more of a pair, if this was possible. If one wanted out (or in), so did the other. Eventually they decided they preferred to be outside in all but the most severe weather. At this time, we had a large screened porch on the river side of the house (actually a 15x30 deck that had been screened in) and we installed a dog/cat door so they could come onto the porch to get food or to escape weather.

They ended up making a bed there and living very happy lives as the official guards.

We lived on a deep water river that emptied into the Chesapeake Bay, but to get to water deep enough for our cabin boat, our dock had to be pretty long. We soon discovered that this pair liked to get up very early every morning and march down to the end of the L-shaped dock. There they would sit together and quietly watch the sunrise come up over the river to the northeast. When the sun was up, they would march back. They did this nearly every day.

Our bedroom also overlooked the dock and the
river, so we began to stretch up in bed and watch
this spectacle. We found that Stewart was the
leader; he also decided when to leave, and Midge
would be right behind. When we had snow, this
routine did not vary, they sat in the snow at the end
of the dock and patiently awaited the sun's
ministrations. And left telltale footprints up and
down the dock.

Eventually this became so much of a routine that we no longer paid attention. Like so many things in life, the astounding became commonplace through sheer repetition. But, oh my, those two were like one.

There came a time when Midge started showing her

age, little things like grey hair and a slowing down. Stewart remained one of the most robust cats we'd ever had, in the peak of health. Then Midge had a series of episodes – probably strokes – and several times she did not know us, and sometimes forgot to eat. Then one day they both left, and never returned. No sign of either was ever found. I think that Midge went into the woods to die. But Stewart? He was in magnificent health. What happened to Stewart? We'll never know. But I know one thing – Stewart would not have abandoned his lifelong friend. I think they are still together.

George and Gator

When Harry left us so suddenly, we knew we had to replace Mom's kitten, so I asked friends and relatives and got a hint about a batch of kittens way out in the country looking for homes.

Mom decided that the kitten would be named George. So I drove up the peninsula, took a ferry, and eventually found the place. They had a Mom cat and her kittens in an outdoor kennel, really just a long box. When I looked in, Mom cat came out and departed in search of food. "Anybody want a home?" I inquired of the bunch in the back of the box.

Only one tiny kitten came forward, all the way to the outside daylight. "You're it", I said, "I guess you want to come home." So George, who fit easily in my palm, got in the car with me for the return trip. I put her in a cat carrier, but she loudly complained and I soon let her out and she was quiet – and didn't try to run all over the car (she's still that way).

Only one small problem – George was a girl. Mom was surprised, but I insisted that the kitten who came forward had to be the right one. I suggested "Georgy Girl", but Mom refused to change the name. So George, the girl, remains George.

J. R. was happy to have a kitten in the house and playtime again. George's ancestor's must have studied aerobatics, because she was happiest chasing things in the air. Any flying bug that came within wildly optimistic range, she would leap and smash her front paws together. And it was truly impressive when she did this while executing a backwards somersault – which she did regularly at an altitude of about two feet, flawlessly landing on her feet. She didn't do it much after she got to be about three years old, but it remains a vivid memory to us. I've never known another cat to do this.

She and J. R. became not only best friends, but nearly inseparable, following each other around the house and out the cat door. They slept together, bathed each other, ate out of the same dish at the same time. I believe she really kept J. R. young at heart as he aged and his health conditions became worse. They never left each other's side. When J. R. could no longer roam the outdoors, he rested in a shady spot where he could watch George's wanderings, and come in when she was ready.

After J.R. left us, we knew we didn't want George to be an only cat. She was completely used to having a best friend who would wash her, sleep with her, play with her, etc. So on a winter trip to Florida, we found a baby kitten whose father was part Maine Coon. The family giving away the kittens put this tiny, all black thing with longish fur in one of my hands, where it promptly fell asleep. "I've never seen him do that before," the owner said. So we invited Gator (as we named him – after all, he is a Florida cat) to come back with us to our Florida apartment to make friends with George.

Now the fun began. Kitten Gator is as wild as his name. If there is to be one word to describe him, it would be irrepressible. He immediately attacked George for fun, despite the fact that, on arrival, she was at least ten times bigger. He would arch his back, stand on tiptoe to look as big as possible, then dance sideways with little hops until within range, then wrap his front legs around her neck and wrestle her to the ground. Of course George, having a major weight advantage, would soon turn this around. Curiously, while George would complain loudly, Gator never made a sound, whether he was attacker or attackee. Completely fearless; made for sport.

Gator at 12 weeks

It took George a couple of weeks to get used to this very violent interloper, but we kept reminding her that she did the same thing to J. R. Before long she was into the spirit and chased as often as she got chased. Meantime, Gator looked for other ways to have fun. And there were lots of opportunities –

bath tissue that unrolls, Kleenex to chew,
unsuspecting humans to bite while trying to sleep,
furniture that needed trimming, and on and on. All
while growing like the proverbial weed.

George and Gator

My wife weaves high-end women's clothing – we follow the fine art shows on the west coast of Florida in the winter, and we installed a loom in the Florida apartment to supplement the looms at home. Do you get the picture? A loom, lots of yarns around. A kitten and a ball of yarn? Boxes and boxes of yarn? Of course, we have to train our cats to keep the loom, the studio, and the yarns off limits. With Gator this was not easy.

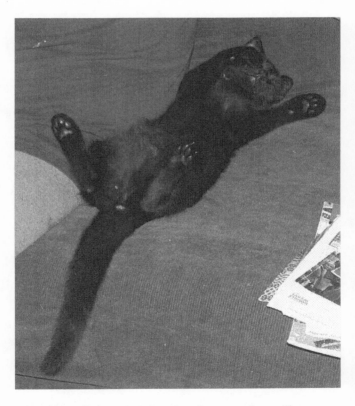

Watching Gator grow up has been truly endless

entertainment. He prefers to sleep completely upside down with all four paws in the air. He sprawls on the furniture that way, and you can't look at him without laughing. And when Mom picks him up and turns him upside down in her arms, he immediately falls asleep. "It's like one of those dolls that turns off when you turn it upside down," she says. Never fails. Or, on our bed, just let him turn over and it's lights out. A most unusual kitten. As I write this, Gator is now a year old, just about full size, and peace reigns in the house. We frequently have a two-cat bed. He is much calmer but does not communicate yet (not counting every night when he loudly announces his entry around 2 a.m.). George does communicate, when it suits her. He still sleeps upside down. And now George is starting to do the same.

Cat DNA

The DNA of a cat is more than 99% the same as
yours and mine. We are very closely related. Yet
there are lots of people who think that shooting cats
is great fun. When asked why, one of them told me
that he liked to watch them "blow up" after being
hit by a large shell. It makes me want to shoot
people like them, which would also be fun, and
improve the gene pool as well.

Cats, like most mammals, have about 20,500 genes.
What is interesting is that the **order** of those genes
in the DNA sequence is almost exactly the same as
in humans. This is not true for any other species.
Other species have a reshuffled genome. Full
genetic maps have now been done of humans, cats,
chimpanzees, mice, rats, and cows. It currently
costs about $50 million to completely map a
species.

Cats are of interest to researchers because they are
so similar to us. They are susceptible to many of
the same diseases as humans, including dozens of
infectious diseases, as well as less common ones
such as diabetes. They are the only animals besides
humans who naturally become sick from immune
deficiency viruses. People get HIV, which causes
AIDS, while the feline immunodeficiency virus or
FIV causes a similar disease in cats. The discovery
of feline leukemia virus in the 1960s led scientists
to realize that viruses can cause cancer. This led to
some of the best smart drugs that we have for
cancer. Cats are also shedding light on a common

cause of human blindness.

Scientists have also used the gene information to trace the common domestic cat back in history to a common ancestor, a particular species of wildcat that still exists in the Middle East. It is now felt that this location was the probable beginning of cat domestication. In this area, man began to settle down into agricultural villages for the first time about 12,000 years ago, developing many domestic cereals and plants. That is about the time and exact same place that cats walked out of woods and did something unusual: act friendly.

Earlier it was thought that the Egyptians were the first to domesticate cats about 4,500 to 5,000 years ago, based on the appearance of cats on Egyptian art and tombs. But then archeologiests unearthed a cat buried with a human on the island of Cyprus (where there were no native wild cat species) that dated to 9,500 years.

The transition of humans from nomadic hunter-gatherers to stationary farmers drew the attention of rodents who fed on the villages' food stores. These pests, in turn, drew wildcats toward this early human society. The cats provided the pest control for the rodents that were attacking the grain stores, as well as providing companionship. Cats were probably not passive in this process; in fact, the so-called "domestication" may have been more the cats idea than man's.

There is good reason to wonder why cats and

humans developed a special relationship. It has been pointed out that cats are unlikely candidates for domestication for a number of reasons. First, other wild animals were domesticated to supply humans with food, clothing or labour, but cats contribute neither sustenance nor work to humans. Second, cats would be difficult to domesticate. The ancestors of most domesticated animals lived in herds with hierarchical structures. Humans simply supplanted the dominant herd individual. Cats, however, are solitary hunters that defend their territory. They are obligatory carnivores and cannot be fed on easily available plant foods. And cats certainly do not take well to instruction. It is therefore highly likely that cats chose humans rather than the other way around as with other domesticates.

This cooperative relationship may explain why domestic cats, unlike dogs and their ancestral relatives, wolves, have not evolved very far from wildcat species. Many scientists feel that this was the most effective biological experiment by an animal. And this co-dependence, each species getting a benefit, is likely why today cats retain their wariness, their aloofness, and their prowess as hunters.

There are differences, though. Because of a gene that remains "quiet" in cats, they cannot taste sweetness. Aspirin is fatal to cats. Cats have more lumbar vertebrae than humans, which allows them greater flexibility (and allows those highly acrobatic maneuvers when falling that helps them always land on their feet). Cats lack the ability to synthesize taurine and require it in their diet. While humans and cats are similar in that both have reduced ability to synthesize taurine in their diets compared to herbivores, the key difference is that cats (who are carnivores) have completely lost the ability and must obtain all that they need of it from their diets. (Humans, as omnivores, have retained the ability to synthesize taurine although it is limited and inefficient compared to herbivores.)

According to various veterinarians, animal therapists, ethologists, and researchers, physiological and behavioral evidence indicates that cats do experience emotions. Emotions expressed by cats include simple feelings of joy, sadness, anger, fear, anxiety, excitement, affection, frustration, pleasure, and contentment. Many people assert that cats display even more complex social emotions, such as compassion, contempt, embarrassment, jealousy, and love.

We are more alike than we are different.

I went into town today on a minor errand, and as I wound my way down the picturesque divided road with palm trees in the divider, I came across a large brown cat lying at the right side, her head against the curb as if on a pillow. She was sprawled on her side extending into the road and was completely still. Obviously she had been hit and killed, although there was no blood or other evidence of collision. Possibly she had been struck in the middle of the road and only made it this far.

Poor beast!

This kind of scene upsets me. Most cats who grow to this size become worldly wise and avoid cars, especially if they live on a trafficked road. Perhaps she recently moved here from a more rural location and had not had a chance to adapt. But I've had my own killed this way – I flash back to Nan leaving her kittens behind – and I've hit a couple myself, including one who had chosen to sleep under my car. With the number of vehicles and drivers, it's inevitable that many animals will pay the price. Still, it angers me that the driver would not stop to see if he could help, or try to contact the nearest house to find the owners – if that had been done, she would not be resting there.

Oh baby beast. I hope you did not suffer, that you went quickly to sleep and dreamed of loving hands around you. I'm sure you were loved. We lost a little light in the world you left behind. I wish it had been me who came up as you were crossing and that I would have been able to let you cross safely. Who among us would not like to be God for a day and stop all the killing and maiming, man and animal alike, or just turn back the hands of time for a day or two or more?

First Dream

In front of the windshield, nothing but grey, solid grey. Not even any motion, yet the ground was only a few hundred feet away and we were at 150 knots, the altimeter slowly unwinding. Having arrived at the IP (Initial Point), I went through my mantra – five T's. Throttle (reduce speed), Time (set stopwatch to monitor 2-minute turns in the Holding Pattern), Twist (set Nav radio to new radial), Turn (to new heading), Talk (report to Approach Control). So I checked in, slowed to 120, ran my mental landing checklist, "GUMP" (Gas, Undercarriage, Mixture, Prop). Set the fuel to the fullest tank, lowered the landing gear (three green lights, all good), pushed the mixture all the way in, to full rich, pushed the prop control all the way forward, then setup 15 inches of manifold pressure at 2500 rpm, a low setting for the descent. I pressed a little more on the right rudder to get the ILS lubber line back in the center. The horizontal line was exactly in the middle, where it was supposed to be. I waited in the greyness, then, a blue light on the center panel and a loud beep. I pushed the thumb switch on top of the wheel and spoke, "Lexington tower, 9193 Charlie, outer marker inbound."

"93 Charlie, roger outer inbound, report the markers" was the brief reply. I verified the rate of descent, retarded the throttle a bit more and thought of Big O, my instructor of years before, saying "most people think the throttle controls the speed and that pulling back the stick makes the airplane climb. It's just the opposite – you can't climb without adding power, so always remember, the stick controls the speed, the throttle controls the altitude." And so it was, once the aircraft was trimmed to fly straight and level, adding throttle made it climb, reducing throttle made it descend, as it tried to obey the trim set and maintain the same speed. Of course, in making this instrument approach, the first thing I did was re-set the trim and slow the airplane, but the basic principle still held true. Outside, rain swept along the edges of the windshield and the grey started to appear ragged, just as I got a yellow light and another beep. "93 Charlie, middle marker." No reply from the tower.

The weather was not forecast to get this bad, but obviously it had worsened to near minimums. I'd be lucky to get in or not have to do a missed approach, and I needed to refuel and continue my trip to Kansas. It felt like it was taking forever but surely it was only a few more seconds until I got a blue light and final beep. "93 Charlie, inner marker".

I expected to get a "93 Charlie, clear to land" but got no answer. Another moment or two and the runway environment swam into sight, powerful lights aimed up from the end of the runway, and then I could see the runway lights themselves as I reduced speed farther, throttling all the way back and easing the wheel into my lap as we ghosted down to 70 mph and sank to the runway. The tower talked to me then and switched me to Ground and I puttered in to the ramp.

It was 1981 and I serviced my consulting clients using a leased Cessna 182RG, a true 200 mph instrument equipped airplane that could carry four people, full baggage and full fuel (87 gallons), which a lot of so-called "4 place" airplanes could not do – many could only take two or three people if you filled the tanks and had normal baggage. A tremendous advantage of the Cessna (and what made it so popular with bush pilots) was that you could fill the cabin right up to the ceiling and still be safe. I often carried three other consultants with me and I could beat the airlines from my house in Ohio to Wichita, because I didn't have to wait for airline schedules or connections or security, and the county airport was 5 minutes from my house.

That quiet night in Kansas, Columbus came to me in a dream for the first time. In the dream I had landed my taildragger – a 1950 Cessna 170, an all-metal 4 place I owned for many years – in the soft grass at a field in the Thousand Islands (a trip I actually made in 1969) and Columbus was my passenger. I tied down the plane and waited for the loaner car and Cols spoke in my head.

– When you fly, you are close.
To what, to Heaven?
– No, to everything. There is no human word for it.
Does this happen with altitude?
– No, it's just a state of mind.

151

Well, I like my state of mind when I fly, unless there are problems. Sometimes single pilot IFR (instrument flight rules) can be stressful due to the pressure of tasks, you know.

– I'm not talking about your mind during stress. It's sort of like an unconscious acceptance. Not something physical. Your mind gets closer to acceptance sometimes when you fly, or after you fly. Not when you are busy with your flying tasks. So, am I supposed to get close, or to get there, or what?

– You have a long way to go, but you will get there.

And will I find you there?

– Yes.

When I awoke, it seemed so strange to have Columbus talk to me in a dream that I wrote down notes.

Home is Where the Cats Are

We were gone for a month, locking the cat door on our Florida home and arranging with a neighbor to come in once a day to check on George and Gator. We filled the feeder and left out water, covered the furniture, and spread out a few toys and cardboard boxes with catnip in them. Crossed our fingers that they would learn to get along a little better…Gator, as a feisty male kitten, was constantly attacking George, the female with the bitchy attitude. The irony was that we had acquired Gator as a companion for George after she lost J.R., since she was so used to a constant companion. And we would go away for days at a time doing art shows, so we thought that George should not be totally alone. But perhaps, forced to share a relatively small space for a long period (doors to several rooms shut, confining them to living room, one bedroom, and kitchen), George and Gator would become more friendly. They could also get to a litter box in garage or bathroom.

So we chased a series of art shows in the mid-Atlantic, worrying, of course about leaving them for so long. They were used to going out the cat door whenever they wanted, prowling the neighborhood with the other cats (lots of them), and would not like being confined inside. But we just could not face letting them roam in a new area (we had moved from NC to FL just 3 months before) with the house empty. A week out, the neighbor called and assured us that they were doing fine, so that was a relief. Were they going to be really mad at us when we got back?

We considered taking them with us, but George hates car travel and we would have to massively change our lodging arrangements (we hoped to stay quite a bit with friends and relatives, some of whom were allergic, some of whom had their own animals not friendly to strange cats). We were also influenced by the fact that we had taken them to Florida for 10 weeks the previous winter…George hated the trip both directions and they were not really happy with the change in environment from what they considered home. When we lived far out in the country, when we traveled we just arranged for someone to check up on them and let them roam in and out of home, but this was a very different situation.

After a long, long month – staying in 10 houses and 3 motels – we finally got back, having decided that this was too long a trip by half and vowing to stick to mostly local shows where we could commute and sleep in our own bed with our own cats! And that is right where both George and Gator headed the night we got back – in bed with us. I showed them that the cat door to the outside world was now unlocked for them, and they went out briefly, but for days they stayed close to us and did not go out for more than a few minutes. They definitely did not want us to be gone that long. But as for getting along together, now George was sometimes washing Gator's head and paws, and they shared the bed while close together; obviously they were better friends (and Gator less aggressive).

After a couple of weeks, George still did not go out much, but Gator was back to long prowls outside at night. He would come in several times a night, always announcing himself, and usually jumping on the bed for a midnight pet before going out again. While he no longer insisted quite so strongly ("pet me or I will bite you"), he still wanted his occasional attention, of course.

We also decided that next time we would travel for a week or two, we would leave the cat door unlocked so they could have normal routines. They don't seem to get in any trouble even though there are probably a dozen cats appearing within a hundred yards of the house. There is an occasional cat disagreement, but as with most cat fights, it is noisy but not damaging. I suspect it is George being noisy because that is the way she is – when Gator leaps, she raises a terrible amount of noise (whereas he is silent, so if he gets in a cat fight I suspect he will assert his powerful muscles and just quietly chomp, grab and hang on – he does it to me!).

So we left for 13 days to do a series of shows, and left the cat door unlocked. We got no less than four calls, one of them in the middle of the night (our cats wear tags with their name and our cellphone number). One call for George (trying to get into the one neighbor's that she knows) and three for Gator. "Is this Gator's owner? He's been camping at our window, would you like to come pick him up?" And "Gator has been camped in our tree, we really like him, he's a very friendly cat."

Gator has been busy canvassing and conning the neighborhood, and has at least three homes who feed him – apparently he makes the rounds in the middle of the night when we are home, and wanted to extend the hours when we were away. One of the neighbors volunteered to keep him until we returned. They enjoyed feeding and petting him, even though they have three dogs. Yes, he's friends with the dogs, too – has never learned to fear anything. What can we do? We have a traveler, not uncommon in the cat/human world. My brother came out of his house one day just in time to see their cat emerge from a neighbor's front door. Each family thought they were the cat's owners.

Now, as I write this, Gator is sprawled across the papers on my desk, right next to the keyboard, and George is in her favorite spot on top of the big laser printer (the altitude advantage!). Hard as it is to get work done – the papers I want are always underneath Gator, and he resists moving or relinquishing papers from under – what could be a better office?

In any case, for many decades it has been our pleasure to come home to our cats. When we returned from a couple of weeks visiting our exchange student's family in Finland a quarter century ago (how does the time go so quickly?), Columbus was waiting for us on the front walk. What could be better than a welcome home from friends with unwavering love and loyalty?

My very occasional communications with George are not very enlightening, so far. Typical, with George leaning against me in bed:

How about talking with me, George?
– Maybe.
Do you like me enough to talk?
– Sometimes. Most of the time it's not worth the trouble.
You're awfully independent…
– And you like to pester me. Bug off.

The Final Lesson

After lots of medical expenses, the tanking of the market and crash of my retirement income investments, and the plunge of the world economy, we had to take bankruptcy and give up our home on the river. A year later, the house still stood vacant. I stopped by for a visit; the grass was not terribly long and the 700 foot driveway protected the property from visitors. Columbus' grave still overlooked the scenic wilderness river, along with Poky and Chili and Zoe, and Harry, all buried by me with loving care next to each other.

I've never been able to accept the concept of "cat heaven" (or any other kind), my logical bent of mind just tells me that when it's over, it's over. There won't be more, and the life that is ended will never be seen again. That may be sad, on one level, but at the same time one could say that heaven – or as much as we can get of it – can be created right here, right now while we are alive. Columbus did make a cogent case for each life being a part of a larger whole, that at least makes sense with my logic. So yes, I guess we return to our biosphere as a whole.

Columbus had a gravestone but it had been set flush with the ground and now the tough mantle of ground cover had grown over it. I knew where the stone was, but could not find it. No matter, Columbus is there, or what is left of his mortal remains. My cancer has metasticized and it won't be long now before I join him, when we are both again part of the whole. I looked down on the long dock and the peaceful river, full of birds and life, and thought about our final communication so long ago.

– Are you ready for the final lesson?
I guess so.
– You have strayed from Life's path.
Are you telling me that I should live a simpler Life?
– Life IS simple. The answers to Life's bigger questions are simple.
Sounds enigmatic. So, should I live like you?
– Humans got off the track. I think it is their big brains, they get easily distracted.
All right, big questions. How about, 'What is Death?'
– It is an ending, of course. But also a merging.
Do you know what you – or I – will merge with?
– Yes. We will both merge with the greater portion of life, the part that surrounds us.
So I suppose we become nothing, and everything, at the same time.
– No. You have not achieved an understanding of Life. Think of it as what the ancients called a mandela. It was shown as a circle because it is never-ending. It repeats, but in a broad sense, not a literal sense.
You mean like reincarnation?
– No, not literally. You and I will be born again only in the sense that everything is born again.
Are you familiar with what humans call Religion?

– Somewhat. I understand there are a great many varieties.

I particularly like the Shinto, Hindu and Buddhist versions, and curiously those are among the most ancient. You know, of course, that many religions provide answers, including the promise of another life.

– Nearly all of them, when they started, were simply pointing to the same truths that we are talking about. They used various stories to point these out. And they tried, or try, to get people who stray to consider a meaningful existence.

What about the existence of God? What about people next to God?

– I suppose you refer to historic people like your Christ or Buddha. They are important inside their specific religions as symbols, or again, as the means to tell a story. They point to the same kind of answers we speak of. As to the idea of God, like the Devil and Heaven and Hell, those are all ideas that are human inventions. Again, started originally for a perfectly good purpose.

You're saying that God does not exist? You are an atheist?

– I can't show you another's existence any more than you can. There may indeed be a higher plane of existence. Neither of us is privy to it. I have not said there is or isn't. Apparently, for humans, the concept is a useful one.

So – in your answer to the question at the end of life – we will cease to exist, and death is emptiness.

– Yes and no. We will certainly cease this existence, and we cannot experience the change in any cerebral way in advance, but we should be sure that it is part of the whole. Just as you are now, a different part of the same whole.

Afterword

I was 28 years old when Columbus was born, and turned 60 shortly after he left us. During this time my children grew up on our old farmstead, moved with us to the shore and started their own married lives. Thus I was privileged to share the central portion of my life with this very, very special cat, and our children had him for company their entire childhood.

People ask me how I could have gone on to have other cats after Cols, and I understand the feeling; there would be no replacing him. At the same time, I feel there is an obligation to treasure his memory by trying to extend the friendship of our species to the continuing members of the cat community, each of which continues to give us love and pleasure, and from time to time, teach us some things.

I like to think that Columbus taught me a few things about interspecies communication, an area that I think we have just begun to explore. Perhaps our abilities will expand to the point where we will go far beyond chimpanzee and dolphin sign language and a few words of language with pets to the point where it will be more common to understand other species' feelings and thoughts. This is already beginning, and I think those who do not recognize the possibilities are sadly limited in their views.

In moments just before sleep, I sometimes hear Cols again. I hope I will walk with him again when it is time for the final sleep. In any case I hope you know by now that the possibility of increased communication is there for you to find.

Sometimes I feel that we are just spectators. We have raised many other cats and dogs from birth to death, and continue to do so, and as this book has demonstrated, I have been fortunate to enjoy a lifetime of cats. But none could compare with Cols. He gave me some enormous gifts and I treasure his memory.

P.S. On the day this book went to press to be proofed, George disappeared. After 24 hours we searched on foot and by car, as she normally would not stay out this long, but saw no sign of her. At 11 p.m. that night, after 30 hours, I heard a noise. I got up and there she was, collapsed just inside the cat door. I told my wife I thought she had a fractured hip and had probably been hit by a car out on Country Club Boulevard, half a block away with lots of traffic. She had dragged herself across the open field behind our house, past the whole length of the house, through the magnetic cat door into the garage, through the garage, through the next cat door into the house, then collapsed. Her fur was full of burrs and detritus from the field.

We dragged her onto a small rug and lifted each end and bore her into our bedroom and put her at the foot of our bed. Next morning we took her to Baywood Veterinary Hospital, where she got a pain injection and X-Rays. Sure enough, the right hip bone was completely broken off the pelvis and separated by quite a bit. Fortunately there was no sign of a ruptured spleen or organ damage, common when this much force is involved. Dr. Smith says she has a better than 50-50 chance of recovery if she is kept in a dog crate for a month to restrict movement, so the bones can knit. However, she will always have a limp.

We took her home with a month's supply of pain pills and the next day, the proof of this book arrived. I decided to add this postscript before approving the first printing. She is doing well so far. I am hoping that you will mentally send best wishes for her to be happily limping around the house. Please drive carefully on Country Club Boulevard and wherever else you go, and let the furred, shelled, and feathered creatures have the best chance.

Footnotes:

1. They made a movie with the same title, but the story bore no relation to the book.
2. tailwheel rather than tricycle gear; tri-gears are easier to handle on the ground but taildraggers are far better for rough field conditions.
3. N9288A; last I checked, it was still flying.
4. I wrote up this takeoff for Flying magazine, "I Learned About Flying From That", #126

About the Author

Lawrence Matthews is now retired and lives with his wife, Shoshana, in Cape Coral, Florida. Prior to this he and his family lived for 25 years on the Pocomoke River on Maryland's Eastern Shore. Before that they lived for 15 years in southwestern Ohio (near Lebanon, halfway between Dayton and Cincinnati) in a big Shaker farmhouse surrounded by barns, pond, and horse trails. Both the farm and the riverbank, he says, were wonderful places to raise children and pets.

He has worked professionally in film and

computers since the 50's, when his still pictures first began to win awards. In the 1970's he helped pioneer the use of large computers to create animated motion picture sequences. In the 90's he began working with digital photographic techniques and custom programming, using his own computer tools to create artwork. Taking advantage of a lifetime's experience in both fields, in 1999 he formed Digi-Art and began offering painted portraits on canvas digitally made from his photographs. His work was the pioneering effort for offering an instant giclee canvas process for portraits.

His degree from Penn State is in Journalism with a minor in Geology. He has produced, edited and directed commercial motion pictures, written countless magazine articles, explored cave systems for the National Park Service and raced sports cars. For some years he was Editor of the NSS News, the monthly magazine of the National Speleological Society (professional cave explorers). He is a Fellow of the Society and served on its Board of Directors. He is an instrument rated pilot and a noted pet photographer.

He still makes prints from his collection of more than 8,000 dog and cat portraits. He has produced portraits at hundreds of dog and cat shows, as well as landscapes, nature, and general subjects. A selection of his images, both photos and paintings, are featured on the website FineArtAmerica.com.

Made in the USA
Charleston, SC
12 January 2014